The People Skills Revolution – I

The
People Skills
Revolution –
Handbook

PAMELA E. MILNE

SOLUTIONS
UNLIMITED

First published in 2013 by Global Professional Publishing
Reprinted 2018

Solutions Unlimited Publishing
20 Birchfield
Sundridge
Sevenoaks
Kent
TN14 6DQ
Email: Pamela.milne@solutionsunlimited.co.uk

ISBN 978-0-9568630-1-0

Printed and bound in the United Kingdom by 4edge Ltd, Hockley, Essex.

With thanks to all those people who developed me while I was busy developing them.

Contents

Introduction

The basic principle behind the People Skills Revolution[1] is that interpersonal skills are cumulative and incremental and that by starting at the bottom with the foundation skills of assertiveness, you will naturally and systematically go on to influence others, negotiate, conciliate, take a stand and finally make peace. The book, which is underpinned by a model called the continuum of interpersonal skills, provides a step-by-step approach to all of these skills. The techniques have proved to be effective both in a coaching environment over a 12-year period and more recently in a written format.

I am very proud of the People Skills Revolution and have gained great satisfaction from the fact that the reader has quick access to all the information they need to improve their impact at a business and personal level, in a highly accessible manner. One reader referred to the book as 'a coach in a paperback'. He and other users of the book have also suggested that they would find it useful to take some of the ideas a step further and to have some examples and exercises to illustrate the ideas presented in the book. When you think about it, this is what would happen in a real coaching environment. I would provide practical illustrations and frameworks to enable people to apply the approaches in their own working and personal lives. Helping people to translate theory into action is the intention behind this handbook.

Just in case you have come across this book without reading the People Skills Revolution, I have tried to make this book a stand-alone publication in its own right, so that anyone picking it up and going through the exercises and practising the techniques would gain as much, if not more, value as someone reading the original book. Building on feedback I have received from readers of the People Skills Revolution so far, I have repeated some important insights and added new thoughts when I thought that would be useful. I have also tried to move some of the ideas forward and taken the opportunity to answer some of the questions that I have been asked about the approach since the book was published.

It has been interesting to see how people have been reading the book. I anticipated that it would be read from start to finish like a story and that people would build their skills in the order that I have suggested. What is clear is that

---

1   Pamela Milne, The People Skills Revolution, Global Professional Publishing 2011

people are using it in a much more pragmatic way and are working on the situations and skills deficits that are bothering them at the time. If I am completely honest, this approach should not have surprised me since that is exactly how I work when coaching clients. First I deal with their immediate presenting concerns whilst keeping the continuum of interpersonal skills model in the back of my mind to help me diagnose the root cause of their problems. Then when they are back on an even keel I go back to the ideas presented in the book to assist them to move systematically up the continuum of interpersonal skills.

In the People Skills Revolution, I deliberately kept information about impoverished behaviour to a minimum in order to focus on the positive skills that can be learnt. It was my belief that the skills of assertiveness would address most of the unproductive behaviour that we take part in and that we experience around us. I wanted the reader to concentrate on the belief that achieving outcomes that at the moment they only dream of were well within their reach.

Having said that, I decided to include a step-by-step approach to defusing the arch-manipulator. I did this since a number of my clients were coming across this behaviour, and despite their considerable interpersonal skills, were having great difficulty dealing with them. The step-by-step approach was worked out in discussions with my clients and proved to be successful in helping them disengage from the chaos that this behaviour brought about. I thought it was appropriate to share the techniques that they had found useful.

The only problem with this strategy is that it seems to encourage people to believe that impoverished behaviour is always brought about by the actions of an arch-manipulator, which simply is not the case. I have noticed that many readers go straight to the back of the book to look up how to defuse the arch-manipulator and I have been sent emails thanking me for writing this section of the book. It is clear that this chapter fulfils a real need for people to understand the impact that the negative behaviour of others has on them personally and the organisation in general.

Having come across arch-manipulators myself, in the past, and helped clients to unravel what is happening to them and their organisations when an arch-manipulator is in their midst, I do still believe that the number of people who behave in this extreme way represents a very tiny proportion of the population. So when readers identify with the experiences and behaviours described in the chapter on 'Defusing the arch-manipulator' in the People Skills Revolution, I believe that they are more likely to have come across aggressive or manipulative behaviour, albeit in an extreme way, rather than characters I describe in the book. I am making this point because I think it can be dangerous to jump to conclusions and label people when they might just have inferior interpersonal behaviour. They may just need to improve their people skills in the same way that you want to in working through this book. In contrast, arch-manipulators study human manipulation like other people might study an art or a science.

There are many gradients of impoverished behaviour, which the skills of assertiveness will help you to respond to. Having said that, it is clear that people have a need to understand more about the situations that lead to conflict and the feelings they experience when they interact with some people who they find difficult to deal with. For this reason, I have included a section on Stephen Karpman's Drama Triangle. This is based on Eric Berne's approach to understanding human behaviour called Transactional Analysis (TA). In his classic book 'Games People Play', Berne highlights how we repeat negative patterns and experience some 'old familiar feelings that we have been here before'. Karpman's Drama Triangle builds on Berne's work by illustrating games graphically in a way that people seem to appreciate and understand quickly without having to know too much about TA itself. I often share this information with clients when they find themselves in conflict, and it seems to greatly increase their awareness and therefore their choices when faced with these dramatic situations.

The good news though is that the techniques I describe to defuse the arch-manipulator and 'game playing', are clearly useful in a wide range of business and personal situations, including those where people are behaving in an aggressive or manipulate manner. In all your dealings with others, try to maintain the 'I positive, you positive' position at all times. If you achieve this you will find applying the ideas in the People Skills Revolution and this hand book much more effective. In any event, whether you are just dealing with a 'difficult' person or an 'arch-manipulator', I believe that assertiveness is the key underpinning skill.

Since I believe that assertiveness is the fundamental building block to all of the skill development strategies outlined in this book, I encourage you not to skip this chapter even if you consider that you have very good interpersonal skills. The reason for this is that when I coach my clients, who mainly work at board director level, if they run into problems with people, the root cause always seems to be lack of assertiveness. This is true, however senior they are in the organisation. It is also clear from my observation that many directors and chief executives can achieve very senior positions without being able to say 'no' to unreasonable requests, harbour a need to avoid conflict, and have a desire to be liked.

I have not met anyone who has not benefited from a greater awareness of the assertiveness tools and techniques, So I encourage you to refresh your skills by reading the chapter on assertiveness even if you consider this to be one of your strengths.

For the ideas in the book to be successful you must also be prepared to revisit your own belief system. Be prepared to acknowledge that your negative thought patterns and your interpretations of the intentions of other people may have undermined your ability to achieve the results that you may up to now have only dreamed of. This book will help you to systematically take away the blocks that prevent you from achieving success – but, and this is a big but, only if you let it. So try to remain open minded about what the book can help you to achieve.

Since writing the book, there have been two main questions that people have asked me. These are 'but don't you think you are teaching people how to be manipulative?' and 'how long did it take you to write the People Skills Revolution?'. I would like to answer these questions here.

Don't you think you are teaching people how to be manipulative?

Actually no, I don't think so. I believe that in the past people with an excellent work ethic and highly developed technical skills have not been able to get the advancement they deserve precisely because they don't have the 'people skills' to influence the decision-makers. As a result they lose out on promotion and are often relegated to the lower levels of organisations, whilst they observe less technically able, but perhaps more people-orientated colleagues getting promotion.

In the People Skills Revolution, I mention the research carried out by Harvey Coleman[2] on how people get recognition. This suggests that only 10 per cent of recognition is gained through performance, whilst 60 per cent is achieved through visibility, and another 30 per cent through the image that people project. When I tell people about these findings, there follows a stunned silence and some rumblings of 'but that's not fair'. Well it may not be fair but when I ask them to consider what actually happens in their organisations compared with what they would like to happen, most people agree that their experience supports the research – those people who are visible and conscious of the image that they project tend to gain promotion over those who just concentrate on doing a good job. So I regard the People Skills Revolution very much as an equalisation process so that the people who do a great job also get the chance to gain the recognition and advancement that they deserve.

In my eyes the fundamental difference between influencing and manipulation is that when you influence with style people want to be around you and support you to achieve your goals. They may even 'trip over themselves' to help you because you are enjoyable to work with and they want to be part of something

---

2   Empowering Yourself – the Organizational Game Revealed, Kendall/Hunt Publishing Company 1996

that is successful. When people are manipulating or aggressive this is not the case. These people use their behaviour to try to get others to do things that they do not want to do that may not be in their best interests. This works in the short term, but in the long term, people either leave or avoid the person who is trying to manipulate or pressurise them. So if you are hesitating to learn how to influence you need to realise that these skills will not only help you to make your life a lot easier but also more productive and fun for the people around you too.

The second question I am asked most often is:

How long did it take you to write The People Skills Revolution?

Well the answer to this is that I started in March and I finished in July. I was able to do this very quickly because I had been using the ideas outlined in the People Skills Revolution, which are underpinned by the continuum of interpersonal skills approach, successfully with my executive coaching clients for over 12 years. So in many respects I was just transferring concepts in my head onto the written page. This is a highly systematic, incremental approach, which has consistent and successful results. When coaching a new client, I just turn up and open my tool kit and get to work. Although I know the techniques are effective, I was not so sure that they would work when the reader just had the written word without the timely and individual support. What is clear, from the feedback I have received since its publication, is that the ideas work in this format too.

Here is some feedback on the book from readers.

'I have had this book for a few months now and found it's supported me making some big changes in my work life and how I get on with people in general.

'Best way to describe the benefit: I'm able to use the book as a portable, always available coach (which helps me find a way to get over issues that have bothered me for years and inspires me to go and do what I really want to do). I've recommended this book to friends and teams I have managed, result – an inexpensive way of instigating a development programme professionally and personally.

'When I look back on when I started using the People Skills Revolution, I realise I am now better paid and have started my own (to date) successful business. I'm better able to identify and handle the "arch-manipulator", be more assertive, influence what's going on and negotiate effectively. Near the end of the book is particularly interesting as I have been inspired to find out what my values are and make the leap and reach for what I used to only dream of.

'Not a bad deal for the price of a paperback.'

'This is an outstanding practical work, which will help you in business, whatever your field is. It is so readable even for the busy executive who doesn't read! There were so many scenarios where I thought this applies to me and I can do something positive. It struck a real chord and has already helped me resolve what used to seem thorny problems.

'I think the book will be an endless source of solutions in your work, with the right profile it should be up there with the greats of influential books for the development of people and business.

'READ IT, APPLY IT, DO GOOD and SUCCEED.'

'This book lays out a step-by-step plan of action to acquiring great people skills that is succinct and to the point.

'I found it inspiring and it made me want to rush out and try the methods on anyone and everyone!

'From corporate arena, to mum at home, everyone could benefit from reading this book.

'If you deal with people (and don't we all?!), this book is a first aid rescue pack!

'A rare book that gets the job done!'

'I really love this book, it spoke to me particularly about eliminating negative self-beliefs and assertiveness using exercises every day, starting to see changes in the way people respond to me.

'No more speaking and not being heard.'

The reactions from people so far are that it is a useful and practical tool, which can be used to change behaviour. As a result of applying the ideas, readers are getting different (and better) outcomes and feeling much more calm, confident and in control in their relationships with others.

I have also been made more aware of where people experience blocks or require additional examples or assistance. The intention of this book is to create a framework to enable readers to learn new skills incrementally and cumulatively from the bottom up and transfer the ideas back into the workplace.

Overview of the People Skills Revolution

When I wrote the People Skills Revolution, I expected people to read it like a novel. The story as it unfolded was intended to demonstrate that change was possible. It was designed to show that provided you changed your beliefs to become more 'I positive, you positive' towards yourself and others, and developed your assertiveness in a step-by-step manner, the gateway would open quite naturally to a wide range of more sophisticated interpersonal skills from influencing to making peace.

From the reader feedback I have received it is clear that some people are pausing at the changing negative belief chapter and not quite believing that they could achieve the positive outcomes that I describe, or they are working through the book and practising the skills as they go along. Either way they are not getting the benefit of knowing that the step-by-step approaches that are described in the book are both possible and achievable if you just step out of your comfort zone to try some different behaviours in a calm, controlled and, most importantly, safe manner.

If you get stuck or go through the book step-by-step, it might take you six months to a year to find out about the skills that peace negotiators used in places in like South Africa or Northern Ireland. It will also take you a while to read about the approach that a Leystonstone cab driver used to help free British hostages who were captured and held hostage by Somali pirates. In the book I make the point that these amazing achievements are just the result of having learnt the basic underpinning skills and having systematically built on them to achieve almost impossible goals. So I have decided to include a succinct overview of the key messages in the People Skills Revolution to motivate you to engage with the concepts presented in the book.

The People Skills Revolution is based on an approach I developed over 12 years ago when I noticed a number of things in relation to my executive coaching clients.

- They were often affected by negative beliefs about themselves, which adversely affected their performance, despite their seniority.
- Time and time again the problems they had in their interactions with people boiled down to a basic lack of assertiveness.
- Once they became more assertive they tended to make rapid progress in acquiring a wide range of people skills.
- Giving them a step-by-step approach to people skills kept them in control of the process and made them want to practice the skills.
- Once they achieved successes in one area of skills they were keen to learn the next set of skills.
- There appeared to be a logical order to the skills people were learning from assertiveness through to influencing, negotiating, conciliation.
- The skills from the levels below formed the cumulative underpinning skills for the next level of interpersonal skills.
- Once I noticed this pattern it was easy to anticipate and develop the next level of skills they were ready to acquire.
- Once people learnt to be more assertive and enjoy their interactions with others, they would then naturally start to acquire more people skills.
- However good their people skills, they still came across people who tried to 'rail road' them into doing something they did not want to do, and they had to learn specific skills to deal with them.

■ When I presented this incremental and systematic build of skills in a model called the continuum of interpersonal skills they quickly understood that the skills they saw in people they admired were not 'god given' but could be learned until they looked natural.

Having developed the continuum of interpersonal skills approach and successfully tested it out, when coaching senior executives, I suspected that there were levels of interpersonal skills beyond conciliation. As a result of reading about highly influential peacemakers I decided to add taking a stand and making peace on to the continuum. I then observed a number of my long-term clients starting to behave in this way.

In my role I have been extremely lucky to have worked with my coaching clients over a long period of time, in many cases years. I could not have developed these approaches without their intelligent engagement, their willingness to try new things and step out of their comfort zone. The feedback that they gave to me about the usefulness of the ideas and concepts has also been invaluable.

Continuum of Interpersonal Skills

Making Peace
Taking a risk to improve society

Taking a Stand
The call to take a stand and follow the dream

Conciliation
The invitation to conciliate

Negotiation
Achieving the overlap in wants and needs

Influencing
Playground not a battlefield

Assertiveness
Expresses needs, allows others to do same

Impoverished skills
Game playing, manipulation, drama

The People Skills Revolution is underpinned by the continuum of interpersonal skills approach, which suggests that interpersonal skills are cumulative and incremental. I propose that these skills can be learnt by anyone with a degree of insight and application in a step-by-step manner.

The hand book will help you to move from where you are now, to where you want to be and will give you tools to get you there.

I believe that what often stands in a our way is not having the skills – although that is certainly a necessary element to success – the factor that most undermines us is our lack of belief that we will be able to achieve what we want to achieve. Once we shift this belief we not only start to get our immediate needs met but we also begin to have dreams and to believe that with the 'wind behind us' we might be able to achieve those dreams.

Having said that, having been someone whose whole mind was awash with negative beliefs and did not even realise that there was a different way to think, I do realise how hard it is to change a destructive belief system. Although the techniques in the book are effective, I am finding that people who read the People Skills Revolution often hesitate at the chapter on changing negative beliefs and do not feel able to go onto the skill building section because they just do not believe that the techniques would work for them. I encourage you to be open minded about the possibility that these ideas work and allow yourself to believe that you can achieve significantly better outcomes in your working and personal life.

Once you believe it is possible to achieve better outcomes through your people skills, the People Skills Revolution Handbook will lead you through the skills of assertiveness, influencing, negotiation, conciliation, taking a stand and making peace in a step-by-step and cumulative manner.

Firstly, I would like you to do a personal audit of where you are now and where you would like to be in the future. Please be aware that these questions look simple but are deceptively deep. Take your time to ponder over the answers and make sure you achieve a balance in your answers between the positive and the negative.

Personal audit

Part 1: Where are you now?

1. What significant events in your life are you most proud of and why? List the events first and then explain why you are proud of this event.

Event   Why

1. _____   _____

2. _____   _____

3. _____   _____

4. _____   _____

5. _____   _____

2. What are the key skills, beliefs or qualities that enabled these events to happen?

1. _____   5. _____

2. _____   6. _____

3. _____   7. _____

4. _____   8. _____

3. After a hard day, what gives you a sense of satisfaction and pleasure?

4. What skills, beliefs, qualities, hold you back from achieving greater success and contentment in your life?

5. What would you consider to be your weak points in relation to your people skills?

6. What elements/behaviours disappoint you about yourself?

7. If you knew what your 'blind spot' was (what other people see and you don't) what do you think it would be?

Negative

Positive

8. What stops you from achieving your goals and dreams?

9. What keeps you going when other people want to give up?

10. Why did you decide to work through the People Skills Revolution Handbook?

Part 2: Where do you want to be?

1. When you get those moments when you believe you are invincible and could achieve anything you want, what do you think about yourself?

2. If you could do something (and knew you could not fail), what would you do?

3. What would you want people to write on your epitaph?

4. If you won a life-changing sum of money on the lottery, what would you do with your life?

5. What would give you satisfaction in your life in
   a) One year from now
   b) 5 years from now
   c) 10 years from now
   d) Your lifetime

Part 3: How are you going to get there?

1. What are the five most important resources, assets, skills and beliefs you have at your disposal to assist you to achieve your goals and dreams?

   1. _____

   2. _____

   3. _____

   4. _____

   5. _____

Reflection: These questions may reveal aspects of yourself that you were not aware of. Hopefully they will also make you realise that you have a significant amount of resources at your disposal to build on. Take your time to integrate your thoughts before moving on to the next section. Jot down any reflections on this exercise below:

Remember: The basic principle behind the People Skills Revolution is that everyone can significantly improve their people skills in a systematic manner. In the process they can start to achieve their goals and dreams in ways that at the moment just does not feel possible. I hope that the personal audit helped you to see where you are now and where you would like to be.

The rest of the book will help get you there.

The continuum of interpersonal skills

The People Skills Revolution approach is underpinned by a model called the continuum of interpersonal skills model, which I have been using to develop thousands of clients, both in a coaching setting and on training programmes since 2000. The continuum is a robust and comprehensive methodology to systematically develop increasingly sophisticated people skills in an incremental, cumulative and step-by-step manner. It works in a one-to-one and group environment, face to face and since the People Skills Revolution was published, it is clear that it also works when following the steps from the written word.

Continuum of Interpersonal Skills

Making Peace
Taking a risk to improve society

Taking a Stand
The call to take a stand and follow the dream

Conciliation
The invitation to conciliate

Negotiation
Achieving the overlap in wants and needs

Influencing
Playground not a battlefield

Assertiveness
Expresses needs, allows others to do same

Impoverished skills
Game playing, manipulation, drama

The continuum of interpersonal skills model suggests that once people become more assertive, they naturally progress to become more influential, interested in negotiating and take on a more conciliatory role.

A smaller percentage of people will also go on to take a stand for what they believe in and become peacemakers.

What reactions did you have to the continuum of interpersonal skills model?

What do you think is the logic behind this approach?

Do you think that this approach will work for you?

Why do you feel this?

What resistance do you feel towards the approach?

What are your beliefs about how successful this approach will be for you?

Reflection: What do your answers suggest about how useful the approach will be to you.

Remember: Writing in 1936, Dale Carnegie, in his book 'How to Win Friends and Influence People'[3], talks about research conducted by the University of Chicago into what adults want to study. The survey revealed that health was the prime interest for adults and that their second preoccupation was people – 'how to understand and get along with people; how to win others to your way of thinking'. People's concern about understanding themselves and how to get along with others remains as true today as it was over 70 years ago.

In fact, with the rise of email, texting and social networking you could argue that the interpersonal skills challenge has become even more complex. Although people look as though they are coming closer together and have more connections than ever before, the quality of the interactions seems to be lower and there is a greater risk of alienation. In this environment it is easy for conflicts to appear out of nowhere and for people to feel very negative about themselves and their ability to have an impact on their environment.

The People Skills Revolution approach will help you to develop positive relationships in the real world.

---

3   Vermillion 2006

The impact of negative beliefs

After working in the field of personal development for many years and having undertaken a Master's Degree in Change Agent Skills and Strategies, I became fascinated by how people change and develop.

The main thing I noticed was that although you can teach people skills you believe to be effective, they will not start to use them and achieve better results unless they believe they will work or more precisely believe that they will work for *them*. I also know this from my own personal experience, which I have highlighted in the People Skills Revolution.

My favourite story about the impact of negative beliefs and our ability to change them, was told by Raymond Corsini in his book 'Current Psychotherapies'[4] when he describes an experience he had when working as a psychologist in Auburn Prison in New York. On the last day of his sentence, a prisoner, comes to his office to thank him for all that he has done for him and for changing his life. Not remembering having spoken to the man he looked at his notes and found that there was only one notation there. It said that he had given him an IQ test about two years before. Asking the man 'are you sure it was me?' the man says 'it was you alright and I will never forget what you said to me. It changed my life'. Corsini then asked him what he had done and the prisoner said: 'You told me I had a high IQ'. In that one sentence the psychologist had inadvertently changed this person's life.

Now I believe that when we are younger we get lots of messages about the way we should be and not all of them are supportive or conducive to forming a positive self-image.

Most of these messages are just habitual thought processes, which are passed along down the family line, which we then accept and integrate into our own way of thinking. If a child is particularly bright or talented it can take a great deal of negative messages to dampen this energy and enthusiasm to ensure that

4   F E Peacock Publishers 1989

they fit into the family or group culture. This negative programming has to be transformed before any progress is made towards achieving the outcomes that learning these new skills will deliver.

I believe that most people experience negative beliefs. Most of us don't know that there is an alternative, nor do we appreciate that other people often suffer the same type of negative thinking as we do.

When reading the book, it is clear that many readers are pausing at the changing negative beliefs chapter as though they don't quite believe that their thinking process can be changed. Let me reassure you that it can. I was recently talking to the son of a friend of mine who was reading the book, and he doubted that I had ever been a negative thinker. I suggested he ask his Dad who had known me for over 25 years whether I had always had a positive outlook on life. He was shocked when his father confirmed that I used to have very low self-esteem.

Our belief system plays a central role in how we see the world and our ability to impact on it.

Are you generally an optimist or a pessimist about your ability to impact on people and situations around you?

What influenced you to adopt this pessimistic or optimistic outlook?

What effect does this outlook have on your life and the outcomes you achieve when interacting with other people?

My key messages from my past were: 'life is hard and it does not get any better' and 'do as I say not what I do'.

What phrases or statements did your family or key influencers use to suggest what you would become or what your life would be like?

How have these phrases or statements impacted on the way you behave in your working and personal life?

If you were to describe a backdrop for your life when you were growing up, what would that back drop or scenery look like, sound like, smell like, feel like?

Reflection: Sometimes it is not easy when we identify the link between the way we were raised and our behaviour in adult life. Consider the answers you have just given and reflect on what they mean to you. What reactions did you have to doing the exercises and how did your responses make you feel?

Remember: 'Whether you believe you can, or you believe you can't – you are usually right'.

Attributed to Henry Ford.

'Any belief can have astonishingly powerful effects as long as it is held with sufficient conviction'.

Jonathan Edwards – British Olympic gold medalist in triple jump 2000.

Transforming negative beliefs

A major element of the People Skills Revolution approach is to become aware of our negative thoughts and to address them as part of the development process.

Beliefs can manifest in many ways but the moment I sense resistance from clients is the moment that I switch from talking about skills and move on to look at the beliefs that they hold about themselves and others. In fact I now believe that negative beliefs have such a pervasive influence on behaviour for more or less everyone, that I always build in a process to engage with them and overcome any negativity they create, as part of the learning process, before going on to develop the next level of skills.

The cycle of negative beliefs

Although I will acknowledge that I have used many different strategies to achieve a more positive outlook, in the People Skills Revolution I highlight the approach that had the biggest impact on me and my clients. This is called the cycle of negative beliefs and was shown to me by a mentor who recognised that I struggled with negative thinking and saw how it undermined my performance.

This is the model he showed me:

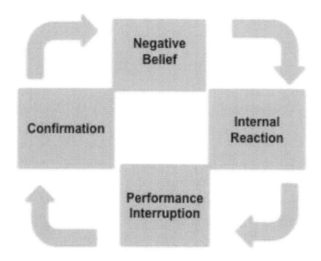

Changing Negative Beliefs

What the cycle of negative beliefs suggests is that we are not born with beliefs, good or bad, they just emerge over time depending on where we decide to focus our attention and the positive or negative groove that we have been brought up with. This approach made me realise that negative thinking is not inevitable.

To demonstrate this process. Suppose one day you wake up feeling that your manager does not like you; you will then look for evidence to support that inkling of a belief, and once you find a piece of evidence it will then reinforce the belief that your manager does not like you.

The next time you are faced with meeting your manager you will focus on the negative belief and the thoughts in your head about that person. This in turn will lead you to perform badly in front of your manager as you concentrate on your negative thoughts rather than focusing on the relationship with the person in front of you. A few times around the negative belief, internal reaction, performance interruption and confirmation cycle, and it will not be long before a possibility of a negative belief turns into an actual negative belief.

In fact, after a few circles around this process, you might start to generate other more destructive negative beliefs, for example 'my manager does not want me around'. This process can explain why we can get drawn into a downward negative spiral about ourselves, and our ability to impact on certain situations or people.

Beliefs are the result of where we decide to focus our attention and you can start the process of thinking more positively just by selecting a more positive belief around a person or situation.

So if you want to start changing your pattern of negative beliefs you first have to become aware of your thought process and how it impacts on your behaviour.

In the People Skills Revolution, I highlight an example of a friend of mine who was prepared to share some of his thought process with others.

He believed: 'What's the point of trying, when I am just to be tolerated initially and then rejected?'

When I asked him what his internal reactions were in relation to this belief, these were his thoughts.

- They are going to find out what I am like.
- I don't like or respect myself.
- I don't believe I am a strong, worthwhile person to be admired.
- I will eventually be rejected.
- I know what I do is to push them away.
- Whatever I do, they won't like me.
- It's not worth trying.
- I always end up in the same place.
- Once they know me, they won't like me.
- They will see that I am a fraud and a liar.
- I play a game to make them like me.
- I can't show myself, because I haven't got anything that they would want.

This is how my friend said that this negative belief interrupted his performance.

- I stare at them.
- I am not brave enough to speak.
- When they speak to me, I try to become what they are looking for.
- I am not real around them.
- I come across more as a clown or tough guy than connecting with the person.
- I don't show the real me.
- I show the bad side of me, so that they will reject me and get it over with.

- I go to extremes – dominant or submissive.
- I can't talk to them.
- I try to be what they want me to be, so I don't get rejected.
- I am nervous and looking for clues that they don't like me.
- I hope that they will hook on to my accent or appearance.
- I am a chameleon. I try out different ways to be.
- I am frightened they are going to see the real me and hurt me.
- I tell them all the bad things.
- I observe myself doing this and think: 'Oh you are doing it again'.
- I react against the impression that you think I am a tough guy.

Having known him for many years even I was quite shocked that he felt this way about himself. I then went on to ask him what he thinks about himself when this has happened and what impact this has on his belief that 'there is no point in trying and he is just being tolerated' when he has behaved in this way. This is what he said, which only served to confirm and reinforce his negative belief:

- They are not interested.
- They don't know me.
- I am a fraud.
- I have never been appreciated for me because I am too frightened.

A few times around the negative belief cycle and it will not be too long before these passing thoughts also start to form the basis of emerging negative beliefs. In this way negative beliefs become self-reinforcing, contagious, destructive and create a downward spiral.

The good news is that this type of negative thinking can be reversed. All you have to do to start the process is to select a more positive belief, which acts as an antidote to the negative belief. You don't even have to believe the new belief; you just have to believe in the possibility of having this belief. The moment you do this, your brain starts to select the evidence to support this new thought process, so after a few cycles around the process, an inkling of a positive belief becomes an actual positive belief, which again becomes self-reinforcing over time.

Creating positive beliefs

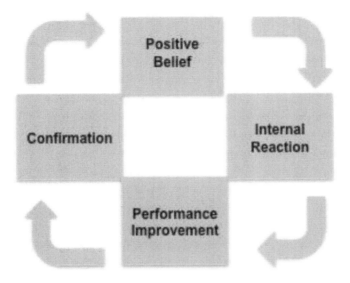

When I did this with my friend around his negative belief that he was 'just to be tolerated initially and then rejected', he selected the new positive belief that 'people will accept me because I am good enough'. This led to the following internal reactions:

- I will feel strong because the basis of any relationship will be built on truth.
- Once people get to know me, they will like me.
- I can show the real me.
- I can accept people liking me.
- I will be happy knowing that I like myself.
- I will be authentic.

Bearing in mind that nothing had changed except his thought process, he was surprised that immediately he felt better and believed that his performance would improve when meeting new people. In fact he thought that next time he would be able to:

- say what I want and need, because I will feel accepted by them,
- not be worried that when I say what I want they will find me out,

- show the real me from the beginning,
- feel safe to express what I want and need,
- be consistent about my needs, be more relaxed, confident and stable,
- be myself,
- face it, if challenged,
- feel I have been set free,
- be free to express myself as I want,
- have a more two-way interaction,
- be more interested in them as a person.

When I asked him what he would think if he had just experienced this type of performance improvement he said he would be:

- out more and talk to more people, to see what happens,
- more productive,
- more confident so that he can talk to people,
- more ready to explore relationships,
- ready to regard the world as a great place filled with potential rather than heartache.

Using this approach he has significantly shifted his negative beliefs about himself and he is using the People Skills Revolution approach to improve his professional and personal effectiveness.

When highlighting your negative beliefs, it is important to bear in mind that you are not creating these negative thoughts, rather you are surfacing them to see what impact they have on your behaviour. It is only when you are aware of these beliefs that you can do something to change them and reverse their impact.

To explore your negative thought patterns first make a list of negative beliefs you are aware of. Here are some, which might trigger your memory:

- They think I am not good enough.
- Whatever I do or say, it does not make any difference.
- I can't do this.
- I am hopeless at this.
- I feel invisible.
- People don't like me.
- I am always rejected.

- People don't listen to me.
- I might as well not be there.
- They think that I am stupid.

Once you have made your list of negative beliefs, use the cycle of negative beliefs to highlight the impact they have on your performance. Whilst it is tempting to just skip this section, I encourage you not to.

Take each negative belief in turn and use the questions below to work through the process. You may be quite surprised to find out what you think about yourself and your ability to impact on others. I guarantee that if you do this at least three times you will identify other negative beliefs that are lurking beneath the surface. Add these to your list and do the process again.

After a while you will be able to identify the negative beliefs without physically doing the exercise but for the moment make your thinking transparent and write down your answers to the questions as you go around the cycle of negative beliefs.

What are your negative beliefs about yourself and your impact on others?

1. _____
2. _____
3. _____
4. _____
5. _____
6. _____
7. _____
8. _____
9. _____
10. _____

Now taking one of the negative beliefs from your list, write it down.

When you have this belief, what is your internal reaction (or thought process) before you have an interaction with a significant person or group?

How does this negative belief and negative internal reaction affect you when you are in the presence of that significant person or group?

When you walk away from the interaction and it has not gone well what do you say to yourself, which confirms your negative belief?

Does this make you aware of any other negative beliefs that you hold about yourself?

Selecting positive beliefs

Looking at your list of negative beliefs, consider what would be more positive beliefs in relation to the people or situations you have just described? (Be sure that the statements are wholly positive and do not include any negatives.)

1. _____
2. _____
3. _____
4. _____
5. _____
6. _____
7. _____
8. _____
9. _____
10. _____

Now starting with the negative belief you have just worked through above, what is your corresponding positive belief?

If you had this belief, what would be your internal reaction (or thought process) before you have an interaction with a significant person or group?

How would this positive belief and positive internal reaction affect you when you are in the presence of a significant person or group?

When you walk away from the interaction and it has gone well, what would you say to yourself, which confirms your positive belief?

Repeat this process for at least three of your negative beliefs.

How would you feel about yourself and your ability to impact on other situations and people if you held these positive beliefs?

Whilst it is tempting to just think about these exercises and not do them, the process of surfacing your beliefs allows you to see what your mind is doing to itself. Exploring how it would feel to have some more positive beliefs has a powerful impact on allowing your brain to seek out more positive experiences, which in turn reinforce the new beliefs.

Reflection: Negative beliefs: When you surface your negative beliefs and their associated internal reactions, it can be quite shocking to discover that you have these thoughts and feelings about yourself that affect your ability to impact on other people and situations. Now take a few moments to consider your thoughts and feelings towards the exercises you have completed in this section.

Positive beliefs: On completing the section on adopting positive beliefs, what are your reactions to what you have written? Pay particular attention to any resistance or sense of optimism that you might be experiencing.

Write down your reactions to the comments you made.

Remember: You are not creating these internal reactions. You are just shining a light on them to become more aware of the impact that they have on your performance. When we have negative beliefs and internal reactions about ourselves, these tend to intrude when you are with other people either on a one-to-one basis or in a group.

Although you are physically present, your mind can be absorbed by observing (and usually criticising) how you are performing, with the result that less of your energy is available to be involved in interacting with the person or people in front of you.

The process of doing this exercise makes you feel more optimistic about approaching the interaction more positively in the future. The outcome may not be perfect straightaway but the process of adopting more positive beliefs will start the self-reinforcing cycle of achieving more effective outcomes.

Impoverished interpersonal skills

Nearly all behaviour is the result of a stimulus and a response, so if you change your stimulus or change your response in a positive way you are likely to achieve a positive outcome in any interactions you engage in. This is one of the basic principles behind the People Skills Revolution approach.

In the chapter on 'impoverished interpersonal skills', I deliberately kept the information simple in order to focus the reader's attention on the positive skills that can be learnt to improve professional and personal effectiveness. I also encouraged you not to take the other person's behaviour personally, and to look after yourself in your interactions with other people rather than concentrate on the behaviour of the other person.

Almost in passing I mentioned game playing, manipulation, bullying and seeing yourself as better or worse in relation to someone else. Towards the end of the People Skills Revolution, I describe the behaviour of arch-manipulators and explain what you can do to defuse the impact of their behaviour.

From the feedback from readers it is clear that many people are going straight to the back of the book to look at the chapter on 'Defusing the arch-manipulator' and telling me how valuable the information has been to them. Although I am very glad that the approach has been useful, I have a difficulty with this idea that so many people are being labeled as arch-manipulators when I believe this behaviour is actually extremely rare.

To balance this I have decided to include another perspective on impoverished behaviour by describing the concept of 'game playing', which from time to time I share with my clients. This information helps them to understand some of the more confusing situations that they find themselves in and to disengage from the dramas that they create. Usually, when we play games, we do this from outside our awareness, so that both parties can become enmeshed in them without understanding what is happening.

Stepping out of the drama involves us in recognising the pattern and making some different decisions about our behaviour. Since games are played out in our unconscious, they can be difficult to get out of, and it can take a great deal of resolve to stop the destructive behaviour, which represents our part in the drama. When one person disengages it usually frees the other player in the game, either to stop doing the corresponding behaviour or to go and find someone else to play with.

On the other hand, arch-manipulators seem to be very conscious of their actions and adjust their behaviour to achieve maximum confusion and impact on the other person. For this reason, although games still represent a complex psychological challenge, it can take an even greater amount of self-awareness, control and skill to defuse the actions of the arch-manipulator.

As you develop increasingly positive beliefs and develop the skills of assertiveness, influencing, negotiation and conciliation, you will become much more aware of and able to disengage from impoverished behaviour.

When you reach the stage of taking a stand you will have a wide range of psychological strategies at your disposal. You will increasingly understand who you are and what you stand for, but you will also have a greater sense of where other people are coming from. You will also notice that you become much less affected by their behaviour and can see past the façade to identify their issues and concerns.

When you are moving towards the point of making peace, it is essential that you understand why people act the way they do. For this reason, I have included the information on game playing and defusing the arch-manipulator in the chapter on 'taking a stand' so that resisting pressure and dealing with these situations becomes a specific set of skills you learn in order to prepare people for the role of peacemaker.

At this point it would be useful to say something about boundaries. In psychological terms, a boundary is an invisible line that defines where one person ends and the other person begins. Quite often in dysfunctional relationships the boundaries between people are blurred. This means that if one person has time, money, services or resources that the other person wants they simply cross the other person's boundary to take what they want.

You can see that some people will be very good at crossing boundaries (having a tendency to be aggressive) and other people will not be good at defending them (having a tendency to be passive). After a while, the boundary will be where the other person sets it not where it should be to protect the individual from the inappropriate use of their time, money, services and resources. The only person who can draw the invisible boundary, let other people know where it is and take action to protect it, is the person whose boundary it is.

From my experience nearly all conflict comes from a lack of clear structure, which allows people to be treated unequally, from holding different perspectives and from a lack of respect of our own and others' boundaries.

The skills of assertiveness greatly assist people to gain a clearer sense of their current boundaries and to consider where they should be. They then enable them defend their own boundaries and to treat the boundaries of others with respect.

At this point in the personal development process, I do not want you to get 'bogged' down with the impoverished skills to the detriment of learning the other skills. Having said that, I think it is helpful to begin understanding impoverished interpersonal skills by looking at what you notice about yourself and the behaviour of others.

Recognising impoverished interpersonal skills

Who do you know who you consider to be a game player, bully or an exploding door mat?

What tends to be the outcome of their behaviour when interacting with others?

What could be a more positive interpretation of their behaviour, i.e. learnt behaviour, negative beliefs about themselves, not having skills to achieve different outcomes, having a bad day, etc?

Which people do you know who continually cross the invisible boundary between themselves and others to have access to their time, money, services and resources?

When might you have been guilty of this behaviour yourself?

Assertiveness

Briefly, assertiveness is a set of skills, which became popular in the 1970s, to assist people to get their needs met in a direct and honest manner whilst allowing other people to do the same. The approach suggests that in order to become more effective you have to change your reaction to a particular stimuli or change your stimuli to achieve a different reaction. In that sense it is an entirely rational and logical process, which aims to take the emotion out of interactions and enables people to remain calm and in control of their behaviour.

Having said this, assertiveness does not discount the role of emotions, since they are important to help us understand why we feel a certain way about a situation. Instead of acting upon emotions, people are encouraged to use them to inform their behaviour and then express their needs clearly and concisely without becoming emotional.

Assertiveness represents a set of skills that enables people to move from a tendency to be passive or aggressive and establish healthy boundaries between themselves and others.

A lot of people, who have a tendency to be passive, when they are developing their assertiveness skills, become concerned that if they start to say 'no' that they will 'run amuck' and won't be able to stop. I want to stress that assertiveness is a set of tools – a kit bag to help you make different choices about your behaviour rather than a personality transplant. It will give you more options and more choices and enable you to remain calm and in control when you want to do so.

People thinking about what assertiveness will mean to them also say the equivalent of: 'But we have to do our jobs don't we?' Well yes you do, but look at it this way. You have two people, and one says 'yes and no' appropriately and the other says 'yes' all the time. If you are a harassed manager who wants to get a task off their desk and on to someone else's, which person would you choose? It is not manipulative to go to the person who is least able to say 'no' – it's just human nature; we would all do it given the opportunity. You will then end up with all the additional work whilst your counterpart is out networking with key players, developing a business opportunity, or booking up their social diary.

People who have a tendency to be passive dislike upsetting people, want to be seen to be part of the team and want to be liked. I believe this behaviour is common throughout society regardless of seniority. At an individual level, it is the person who is impacted by having less time, less money and more stress. At an organisational level, it can be particularly destructive especially in situations when decisiveness is essential.

If a leader cannot say 'no', then lack of assertiveness can result in them dancing to the tune of those with diverse agendas. Their aim of keeping everyone happy means that other people are able to run rings around them. This leaves the way open for those who have a tendency to be aggressive and manipulators to gain power and control.

From my experience as an executive coach and management trainer for the past 20 years, lack of assertiveness seems to be the cause of most interpersonal difficulties, whether the person is a chief executive officer, someone working on the shop floor, or a member of a family.

If you have read the People Skills Revolution you will know how fundamental I believe assertiveness is to the development of sophisticated people skills. In fact I believe they are the basic underpinning skills to all the other skills on the continuum of interpersonal skills. They are also the answer to defusing the very sophisticated strategies used by the arch-manipulator, which I discuss in the chapter on 'taking a stand'.

The basic techniques of assertiveness are broken record, fogging, negative assertion, negative enquiry and giving constructive feedback. There is also an emphasis on using 'I' statements to take responsibility for your reactions and feelings rather than blaming them on the other person.

Another key feature of the assertive approach is the adoption of an 'I positive, you positive' stance in all of your interactions with others. When you think about it, this should not be that radical an idea that you treat everyone equally with the same degree of respect as you would hope to have for yourself. In fact, these elements are often out of balance. We may have a tendency to either adopt the 'I negative, you positive' (passive) position or to take the 'I positive, you negative' (aggressive) position.

To achieve a place of balance you will need to consciously move your thoughts and behaviour to operate from an 'I positive, you positive' position. The skill building outlined in this book is based on the assumption that you have achieved an 'I positive, you positive' perspective in all your interactions with others.

You also need to become much more self-aware of your behaviour and the impact you have on others. In fact awareness is the precurser to making the decision to change any behaviour.

How 'I positive, you positive' are you?

Think about the 'I positive, you positive' position. Be honest with yourself, what is your natural tendency or dominant style? (tick one)

I positive, you negative _____

I negative, you negative _____

I negative, you positive _____

I positive, you positive _____

What impact does this tendency to behave from this position have on your interactions with others?

Would you say that you have a particular tendency to be passive (putting the needs of others before your own), aggressive (putting your own needs before the needs of others) or to swing between the two positions?

What comments about your impact on them have more than two people made about your interactions with them? Be sure to include positive as well as negative comments.

What patterns of comments, positive and negative, have you received from people about your behaviour?

Do you think there is any validity in these comments. If yes, why? If no, why not?

What actions or changes in your beliefs about people would it take to shift your current position to be more 'I positive, you positive?

Give up 'stamp collecting'

When looking at behaviour and how it can become out of balance, the concept of trading stamps can be very helpful. Trading stamps became popular during the Great Depression of the 1930s. They were printed stamps, which were given out when goods were purchased. They could be saved and pasted into booklets until the individual collecting them had a sufficient number to exchange them for a particular item of merchandise.

In the context of human interaction, when someone does something that we feel uneasy about, we often rationalise the situation by saying: 'It is only a small incident and it is not worth bothering about.'

We think we have 'let this go'. But we do not let it go. Instead, each time we are feeling uncomfortable about something that has happened, we collect a 'stamp' and put it in our 'book'. When we have a full book, we 'cash them in'.

This is why an apparently unassuming person can act completely out of character – perhaps screaming at the top of their voice in the middle of the office about something really insignificant. It is not only that incident that they are screaming about. Rather, it is the cumulative effect of all the other incidents that have happened, which they have decided not to act upon (but instead subconsciously collected a 'stamp' about). Often, the intensity of the reaction in relation to the event is not only shocking to colleagues, friends and family, but it can also be shocking to the person who has this reaction, especially if they have a tendency to regard themselves as very passive. Embarrassed by their outburst, they can become even more determined to control their emotions rather than acting on them, making a lack of assertiveness a self-reinforcing circle.

Stamp collecting is the process of collecting resentments about people's behaviour in the same way that you might have collected trading stamps in the past. When you have a full book of resentments you cashed them in for a reward. In the collecting stamps analogy, the reward is the release of anger resulting from the built up resentments in relation to someone or the attention you receive for uncharacteristic behaviour.

Are you a stamp collector (building up small resentments, which then blow up into a bigger disputes)?

What do you collect stamps about in relation to the behaviour of others?

Does a particular person or type of person trigger this reaction in you?

What effect does holding onto the resentment (stamp collecting) have on your behaviour and feelings?

What action could you take to avoid collecting stamps and avoid the situation from escalating?

Identifying your needs

Assertivenss is about getting our needs met in a direct and straightforward manner and allowing other people to do the same. This can sometimes be easy to say but difficult to achieve. Children are good at expressing their needs. If they express those needs and they are satisfied they go on to have other needs. If those needs are not met they gradually stop having needs. Sometimes, if we do not have the ability to get our needs satisfied, it is much easier not to have needs than to acknowledge that we have needs that are not being met.

In order to become more assertive we need to recognise and value our needs. For some people this might involve becoming reacquainted with needs that they gave up on a long time ago.

Here are some common needs:

- To have attention.
- To be listened to.
- To ask for what you want directly.
- To stand up for yourself.
- To say 'no' to people.
- To protect your boundaries.
- To express your feelings.
- To ask people to return things.

■ To express your feelings, thoughts and ideas.

What are your needs?

List three things that you know you need when interacting with others, e.g. to say 'no' to inappropriate requests for money, to speak so that people listen, to be able to request a promotion, to be able to express your ideas, to be respected, to ask for things you want, to be able to act on your feelings.

1. _____

2. _____

3. _____

How do you ensure that you get your needs met?

If your awareness of your needs is a bit shaky, what could you do to become clearer about what they are?

What needs do other people have that you wish you had? This will help you to identify needs that you have but may not be aware of. These might be issues such as being able to say 'no' when people ask you to change shifts, asking people to do something for you, or challenging people when they have done something you are not happy about.

1. _____

2. _____

3. _____

What would you like to change about your interactions with other people?

What specific words or phrases do people usually use to deflect you from your intention to get your needs met?

How do you feel when they manage to deflect you off your intentions and you feel that the same incident or event has 'happened again'?

If you do 'stick to your guns' and get your point across, how do you feel after the event?

To avoid the weakest link being you, you have to learn to identify and protect your boundaries – the invisible line between where you end and where other people begin. How can you do this?

Using assertiveness skills to get your needs met

We all have needs and have the right to get those needs met. The skills of assertiveness will give you the strategies to stop putting the needs of others before your own needs. Once you learn to do this you will start to reconnect with your own needs and be able to develop the interpersonal skills to get your needs met on an increasingly regular basis.

Alternatively if you habitually tend to put your needs above other people's, it will assist you to more to a more 'I positive, you positive' position. Moving from a tendency to be aggressive to a more assertive position is the more difficult transition. The reward is people wanting to be around you, rather than them clamoring to leave the room when you come into it.

In an attempt to avoid upsetting people, or wanting to be liked, those with a tendency to be passive tend to give too much background information, make excuses, offer explanations and make too generous offers.

Providing too much information, creates an opportunity for the other person to take control of the conversation, by 'hooking' on to what you have said. They can then turn the discussion back onto their needs and agendas rather than yours. Equally do not feel compelled to follow up or respond to flattering or critical remarks, which are intended to deflect from your resolve to get your needs met. People are much more predictable than you think. As a general rule, a person who wants to deflect you from your intention to become more assertive will usually use flattery first and if that does not work they will criticise you.

The moment you respond to one of these deflective 'hooks' and follow that line of conversation, is the moment that you have lost control of the interaction.

A step-by-step approach to assertiveness

To keep in control of assertive interactions, I suggest you use the following step-by-step approach.

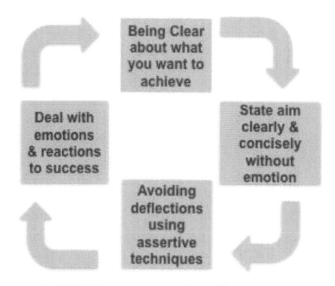

- ▪ **Step 1:** Be clear about what you want to achieve
- ▪ **Step 2:** State your aim clearly and concisely without using emotional language or behaviour
- ▪ **Step 3:** Avoid deflections using the assertiveness techniques
- ▪ **Step 4:** Deal with your own emotional reactions to being successful

The assertive tool kit

The basic assertive tool kit, includes the techniques of:

Broken record

A prepared statement expressing your aims, which you would feel comfortable to repeat a number of times. This idea of repeating the same statement helps you to keep your sense of focus by constantly coming back to your purpose without allowing others to deflect you. To avoid sounding too much like a broken record, this technique works best when combined with other techniques rather than used in isolation.

Fogging

Enables you to allow the critical words of others to 'hang in the air' without needing to defend or attack, acting like a fog bank to their comments, by saying phrases like 'I can understand why you might think that'.

Negative assertion

Allows you to accept and acknowledge that we all make mistakes.

Negative enquiry

Encourages you to request more specific information from people making critical remarks, for example 'what is it specifically about my behaviour that is causing you a problem?'

Giving constructive feedback

Useful to confront behaviour that you observe in others, which has a negative impact on you and enables you to avoid the process of 'collecting stamps'.

Assertiveness – a practical example

Imagine you are the director of finance in an organisation facing severe financial constraints. You are due to meet a department head about a new project he is championing and you know he will ask you for funding.

The board has agreed that no further expenditure should be made without a comprehensive business case, but you know that this person can be aggressive or manipulative. You also know your own tendency to want to be liked.

Step 1: Be clear about what you want to achieve

Make the decision that the next time you are approached to approve additional funding, you will say 'no'. Consider how you will express this to the person who makes the request

Step 2: State your aim clearly and concisely without emotional language or behaviour

Prepare a statement, which you will be comfortable saying (like a broken record) whenever your resolve is challenged.

So when the department head introduces the subject of the new project and asks you directly for funding, you then state your aim clearly and concisely that you must have a business case for additional funding to be approved.

For example: 'Although I understand your point of view, the board had agreed that no further expenditure should be approved without a comprehensive business case'.

So far so good. But then the aggressive or manipulative departmental head starts trying to deflect you from your purpose.

Step 3: Avoid deflections using assertiveness techniques

In order to avoid the deflections from the department head, the conversation might go something like this:

> **Department head (DH):** *'You have always been so supportive of this department and the quality of our work has improved so much as a result – it certainly seems to have earned you positive press coverage…' (Flattery)*
>
> **You:** *'Thank you, I appreciate the compliments, but – as I said before – to justify more funding for your department, you must have a business case.' (Broken record)*

DH: *'Oh dear, have you become such a weak leader these days that you are afraid of your own shadow and feel compelled to kowtow to the organisational "powers that be"?' (Criticism)*

You: *'I know it might seem that way sometimes, but to agree expenditure I need a business plan.' (Fogging and broken record)*

DH: *'Well I must say, you have become a shadow of your former self.' (Criticism)*

You: *(by now you are probably a bit put out by these comments, but you are also aware that going on the defensive, or on the attack, will probably lead to an argument and result in your losing control of the interaction): 'I can understand that it may seem that way to you these days.' (Fogging)*

DH: *'It's just ridiculous, you have just sprung this idea on us without any notice. You do realise that we have a business to run here?'*

You: *'Yes, I would have liked to have given you a bit more notice.' (Negative assertion)*

(Most people would just give up at this point, since you have not risen to the bait, but the DH carries on in the same vein of criticising and insulting you.)

You: *'What exactly is it about me asking you to do a business plan that is causing you problems?' (Negative enquiry)*

DH: *'I don't have the expertise for doing business plans'; or 'This funding requirement is too urgent for lots of paperwork.' (Whatever the response to your negative enquiry, it enables you to see that either the DH's comments are manipulative or they just need further assistance to comply with your request.)*

Step 4: Deal with your own emotional reactions to being successful

Finally it is possible that the director of finance might feel guilty, uncomfortable or affected by the threats after achieving his goals.

This is entirely to be expected. It is important to remember that in the time it took to assert his needs clearly, calmly and honestly, he will have prevented the department head from acquiring additional funds through aggressive behaviour.

And remember, if anyone has ever said 'no' to this type of request, in similar circumstances, it will be possible for you to say 'no' to this type of request. You just have to learn the skills to do this with a sense of style.

When we move out of our comfort zone, by definition it often feels uncomfortable. This is a healthy sign. The more you stay just slightly out of your comfort zone – in your risk zone – the more comfortable it will start to feel. After a while, being able to be assertive in challenging circumstances will just become part of the way you operate. In the process you will have prevented other people from having unreasonable access to your time, services, resources or budget.

Planning an assertive conversation

List below 10 situations when you would like to become more assertive.

1. _____

2. _____

3. _____

4. _____

5. _____

6. _____

7. _____

8. _____

9. _____

10. _____

When becoming more assertive it is better to start on situations with a low level of risk – for example saying that you do not want to attend a particular social event would likely be a low risk for most people. Then work up the list increasing the level of difficulty each time.

If you practice assertiveness techniques on low-level risk interactions, experience the discomfort whilst achieving success, you will then be able to gradually develop your people skills muscles by moving on to the next level of difficulty on your list.

In order to change our behaviour we need to step out of our comfort zone, which by definition will feel uncomfortable. The trick is to work at the cusp between your comfort zone and risk zone. After a while, the more you step out of your comfort zone, the more you will begin to feel more comfortable in your risk zone until your comfort zone gradually increases.

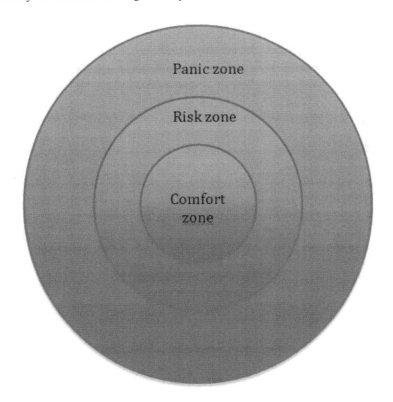

When people try new behaviours that feel unsafe for them and lead to negative outcomes, they not only panic at the time but then jump back into a smaller comfort zone, which will then shrink as a result of the experience.

The step-by-step approaches in this book will prevent you from stumbling into your panic zone and will lead you safely, gradually and incrementally to develop your skills, allowing each success to build on previous success. After a while, when each level of the skills are included in your expanded comfort zone, your behaviour will appear very natural not only to yourself but also to others.

Step 1: Be clear about what you want to achieve

From your list of 10 situations where you would like to be more assertive, pick one (with a medium level of difficulty) that you would like to change?

What more positive outcome would you like to achieve in this interaction?

How could you use the tools of assertiveness to approach this situation differently?

Step 2: State your aim clearly and concisely

What could you say to state your needs without showing emotional behaviour or using emotional language?

Write down a phrase that sums up your assertive position, which you would be comfortable repeating a number of times (like a broken record) if someone tried to deflect from what you want to achieve.

Step 3: Avoid deflections using the assertiveness techniques

You have already fixed your aim clearly in your head and have constructed your assertive statement to express your needs clearly and concisely without using emotional language or behaviour.

Now with the situation you would like to change in mind, what 'hooks' would you imagine the other party might embed into the conversation to deflect you from your intentions to be assertive?

Some common phrases to watch out for are:

Flattery

> *You are the expert in this field. No one will give me better advice than you can.*
> *You have always been so reliable, friendly or helpful in the past.*
> *I tell everyone how wonderful you are.*
> *I know I can rely on you to help me.*
> *Can you change your arrangements for me since you have helped me out before?*

Criticism

> *If this is not done by this afternoon my job is on the line (or your job is on the line).*
> *But there is no one else to help me.*
> *I am relying on you.*
> *You are being very aggressive.*
> *I might have to report you, you know.*
> *What do you mean you are not going to do it?*
> *But I thought you were my ally.*
> *You have to do it, it's got to be done today.*
> *You do know your appraisal is coming up shortly don't you?*
> *I am very disappointed in you.*

List below what phrases or words you imagine the other person might use to deflect you from your intention to be assertive.

Anticipated deflections

1. _____
2. _____
3. _____
4. _____
5. _____

Using the assertiveness techniques of broken record, fogging, negative assertion and negative enquiry, plan an assertive response to all of the deflective statements that you have anticipated.

1. _____
2. _____
3. _____
4. _____
5. _____

Step 4: Deal with your own emotional reactions to being successful

In asserting yourself it is likely that you will feel guilty or uneasy, at least in the first instance. Alternatively, you may not have got your needs met (when you usually do) because you have been assertive rather than aggressive.

How would you deal with these outcomes?

What would you do about feeling guilty?

What would you do about not getting your needs met in the way you have become accustomed to?

If you have had a tendency to be passive and have been successful in getting your needs met, you may feel guilty. If you have had a tendency to be aggressive, you may feel a sense of dissatisfaction when you have allowed others to get their needs met. What would be the benefits of living with these feelings of unease for a short while?

How do you feel about the possibility of getting your needs met when this might mean not meeting the needs of others?

How would you feel if you gave up getting your needs met (because you have a tendency to be aggressive) in order to enable other people to express and meet their needs?

Taking action – assertiveness

Having planned your more assertive interaction, try it out in a real situation.

What actions do you have to take to make this conversation happen?

What is stopping you from having this conversation?

What can you do to overcome your resistance?

When would you be able to have this conversation?

DO IT!
Report back

What happened when you had the conversation with the person you wanted to be more assertive with?

What went well?

What did not go well?

What would you do next time to build on the aspects of your performance that went well?

Work through your list of 10 situations where you would like to be more assertive, increasing the level of difficulty each time.

Giving effective feedback

Once you are successful in becoming more assertive you become less enmeshed in your own thought processes and begin to become more aware of the behaviour of others. Much of the less productive behaviour of others can be modified by using the assertiveness techniques.

However, when you start to notice that you are 'collecting stamps' in relation to another person's behaviour, it may be useful to give them constructive feedback rather than allow the build up of resentment to continue.

Most people do not find this very easy. They are concerned that it might go horribly wrong or it reminds them of when they have received unpleasant criticism in the past. If you think about it though, it is a very basic life skill and most of our significant development has come when someone has had the courage to tell us something about our behaviour, in a calm and controlled manner, which we might have preferred not to know. Giving constructive feedback becomes most effective and safe when it is:

Structured	Respectful
Recent	Owned
Specific	Unemotional
Descriptive	Non labeling

Factual

Timely

Private

Non-judgemental

Focused on behaviour not personality

Constructive feedback – a structured approach

The following constructive feedback approach will keep you on course and avoid the conversation leading to conflict.

- Stage 1: Explain the situation
- Stage 2: Explain why you think you need to raise the issue
- Stage 3: Outline the impact that their behaviour had on you, the team, the business or other relevant parties
- Stage 4: Pause for a response or invite a reaction
- Stage 5: Describe what you would like them to do differently from what they are currently doing
- Stage 6: Explain how this will improve the situation
- Stage 7: Ask them to comment on your suggestion or make alternative ones

Giving constructive feedback – a practical example

Stage 1: Explain the situation

You: *'Last Tuesday I noticed that you were 10 minutes late for work. I also noticed that on Thursday you were 20 minutes late for work.'*

Stage 2: Explain why you think you need to raise the issue

You: *'I need to mention this, because it had an impact on the rest of the team and detracts from the level of service that we are able to provide.'*

Stage 3: Outline the impact that their behaviour had on you, the team, the business or other relevant parties

You: 'Sarah had to stay on late to cover for you and Mike missed his appointment at the Regional Office. You will remember that Stella and Sarah both rang you to find out where you were, but your phone kept going to voicemail. In addition, a number of your clients rang up asking for you and we were not sure when you would be in.'

Stage 4: Pause for a response or invite a reaction

You: 'I wonder if you have any comments to make on what I have just told you?'

The most likely response is that they will either defend or attack. They will either say the equivalent of:

Them: 'It was only a few minutes and I don't know what you are bothering about. Everyone does it from time to time and when you interviewed me, you did say that you valued flexibility within the team. I was just being flexible.'

Or they might be genuinely surprised that you are raising it because they really did not know that it was a problem. They will usually mumble something like: 'But I didn't realise it was a problem.' If this is the case, you will know that they have heard you and they are generally ready to accept that you may have a point.

If they continue to defend or attack, even when you bring them back to the point, you might want to restate the impact of their behaviour whilst at the same time valuing the elements of the task that they are doing well.

Allowing them to 'let off steam' at this stage until they have finished, then calmly and gently bringing them back to the point, will prevent them from ranting (and therefore taking control of the conversation) at the end of the feedback process.

Which ever response you get, you are now ready to go on to the next stage.

Stage 5: Describe what you would like them to do differently from what they are currently doing

You: *'I need you to be here on time, but if you are going to be late I want you to ring Sarah and let her know the reason you are late and when you will arrive.'*

Stage 6: Explain how this will improve the situation

You: *'This will enable other people to get on with their work and not have to spend time reorganising their busy schedules.'*

Stage 7: Ask them to comment on your suggestion or make alternative ones

You: *'Have you got any comments to make about this suggestion?'*

Then give them the opportunity to comment on what you have said and perhaps come up with other strategies.

Planning a 'giving constructive feedback' conversation

Who would you like to give constructive feedback to and why?

Be specific about their behaviour and how it affects you.

What would you like to be different about their behaviour?

If they started to question your general attitude towards them and their performance, what could you say to reassure them that they do other specific elements of the job well but reinforce that this particular behaviour has a negative impact?

Use the framework below to plan what you would say to give feedback.

1. When you did this

2. I felt or thought

3. And it had this impact on me, team, business, etc, ………..

4. Pause for discussion – use this space to guage their reaction to what you have told them. This will enable you decide whether you need to repeat or reinforce stages 1-3 or whether you are able to go straight on to steps 5-7.

   When you raise this issue with them you are likely to get one of two reactions – either 'its not just me – the others do it too' or 'oh I did not realise'. What is their most likely reaction if you raised this issue with them?

Plan your response to their likely reaction to ensure that you are not deflected from your intention to give feedback.

5. What I would like you do next is

What would you like them to do differently next time this situation arises?

6. Because .... explain how this would improve the situation

How would this improve the situation?

7. What are your thoughts on what I have suggested?

What can you say to encourage them to comment on or discuss your suggestion?

Giving praise

Receiving specific, sincere, descriptive praise sometimes seems like a rare commodity. Often people who have done good work just 'waive it off' by saying 'I was only doing my job'. However praise and recognition can be a huge motivator and generally, if you tell people that you like what they are doing, they will keep on doing it. Then they will often look for other ways to improve their performance.

List below three people who do things that you value, and use the approach above to give them praise regarding their behaviour and what you think they do well.

1. _____

2. _____

3. _____

Taking action – giving praise

Having planned your 'giving constructive feedback' and 'giving praise' conversations, when will you step out of your comfort zone to do it (be as specific as possible about who you will talk to and when)?

DO IT!
Report back

What happened?

What would you do differently next time?

Reflection: Reflect for a moment on your comments about identifying your needs and getting your needs met. What reactions did you have to doing this section and how did completing the questions make you feel?

It might come as a surprise to you to know that you collect stamps about situations or people when you may consider yourself to be a very easy going person. What are your thoughts on the answers you have given in this section?

What are your reactions to using the tools of assertiveness in your own work or personal life situations? Reflect for a moment on your answers.

How do your answers make you feel?

Giving constructive feedback to people can be challenging, especially if you have not really done it before. How did answering the questions in relation to giving feedback make you feel?

When you gave feedback to someone, how did it go?

What progress have you made in developing your assertiveness skills since starting this chapter?

Remember: This can be one of the most difficult sections to complete since you may have to confront the thought that you stopped having needs because you lacked the skills to get your needs met.

It is not easy to reflect on who we are and how other people see us. We tend to see and hear comments, which reinforce our view about ourselves.

Make sure your reflections include all the positive comments that people have made about you and your impact on them. Then reflect on what you have learnt about yourself in answering these questions.

It is only when we are more aware of our behaviour and understand why we do things that we can begin to change our reactions to people and events. Awareness is the precursor to change, so although it may be uncomfortable to find out about some hidden aspects of ourselves it is exactly this process that enables us to make different choices in the future.

Some people may not know what their positive or negative stance is in relation to others. This is because our behaviour, and the impact we have on others, may be outside of our awareness. Patterns of comments from more than one person can give a good clue to how others see us.

Individual comments about our behaviour can often be unhelpful and may just be 'hooks' that some people use to deflect us off a course of action that does not suit them.

This section is about using tried and tested assertiveness techniques to achieve your goals and avoid being deflected off your path by other people.

Once you become more assertive you may be surprised to realise that you may be criticised more than before. Receiving criticism like this can be difficult for the person who likes to be liked and wants to be recognised as the person who does a good job. When working with clients who are improving their assertiveness skills, they often feel they are not progressing when they get criticised, when in fact the opposite is the case.

To be criticised (when you are not usually criticised) suggests that the other person is beginning to notice your resistance. You have not responded to flattery and you are standing your ground more. Learning to deal with criticism is just part of the process of becoming more assertive and resisting what might be the unreasonable demands of others.

Moving out of your comfort zone is, by definition, uncomfortable. Until you learn to do this your comfort zone will not expand. So sit with the discomfort for a while and know it will pass. All learning involves a degree of mental stretch and discomfort.

A great deal of our own significant learning comes when someone has the courage to tell us something about our behaviour that we might not like to hear. Since most of us do not like to be told about the negative aspects of our behaviour and how it affects other people we have a natural tendency to try to deflect the conversation or change the subject. When giving people feedback you need to anticipate what the other person might say to sidetrack this conversation. When you have this conversation with someone, if you get stuck or side tracked go back to the model, work out where you were in the process and start again from there.

If you have completed these exercises and tried them out in real work or personal life situations you will have stablised many of your interactions with other people and gained more control of your time, resources and corporate or personal wallet.

You are ready to build on your new insights about yourself and to develop the more advanced skills outline in the book. This will enable you to achieve more positive outcomes in your work and personal life.

Influencing

If you have developed your assertiveness skills, and have achieved some success, you will feel much more confident, calm and in control of your behaviour. Now it's time to play. In this chapter you will start enjoying what you can achieve with your people skills.

It is a well-known adage that 'people do things for people'. So if you want things to be done for you, move away from the idea that it is your role that dictates who does what for you and when. You must get to know the people you want to influence and then present your request at a time and a pace that matches your relationship.

Let me restate here that influencing is not the same as manipulation. People who are manipulative want to achieve their goals at any cost, regardless of what other people want. They will try lots of different tactics to get people to agree. I think the reason for our concern about becoming manipulative is that we really dislike it when people manipulate us, and would prefer not to get our needs met at all rather than to treat people in this way.

When you are influencing, people enjoy working with you and often go out of their way to help you voluntarily.

In the People Skills Revolution, I present a step-by-step approach to influencing that works and allows you to stay in control of the process.

Recently talking to a colleague who was consciously and successfully using the skills, he surprised me when he said he kept on thinking about the approach and found himself asking: 'How can things be that simple?' He also began to observe when others demonstrated the skills and when they didn't, and noticed what a difference this made in the outcomes they were able to achieve.

Before starting to learn the step-by-step approach, consider someone you admire who you regard to be influential and inspiring. Who are they?

What qualities and characteristics do they display?

I hope you can see that all these qualities and characteristics can be learnt and you will significantly increase your impact on people once you develop the skills of influencing.

Here is the four stage, step-by-step model I suggest you follow to develop your ability to influence others:

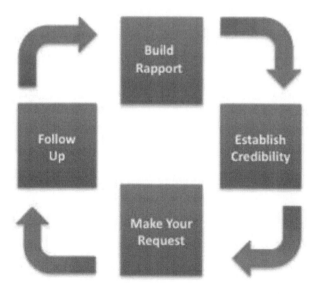

A Step by Step Approach
The Cycle of Influence

Build Rapport

Establish Credibility

Make Your Request

Follow Up

- **Step 1:** Build rapport in order to make a connection with the person
- **Step 2:** Establish your credibility (or why they should listen to you)
- **Step 3:** Make your request simply and clearly to encourage a 'yes'
- **Step 4:** Follow up and thank them for their assistance

Influencing: a practical example

Below is an example of the cycle of influence in action, with a head of training and development wanting to influence the director of human resources to enable the service to move from a provider of stand-up training to a more internal consultancy role. In this example the head of training and development is going to influence upwards to the director of human resources. They do this by addressing their agendas and concerns for introducing change, concern for customers as a group, improving systems and procedures, and implementing strategic initiatives.

It is important to say that they have a good working relationship and they have built rapport with each other over a period of years. What they know about each other is that the head of training and development loves to travel to exotic places, is a member of a band and is on the board of governers for their children's school.

On the other hand the director of human resources enjoys sailing, supports Manchester United and loves photography. The two managers meet for lunch, coffee or after work on a regular basis, just to catch up and chat about issues of mutual interest. The head of training and development notices that his colleague is in a relaxed mood and thinks that this might be a good time to mention about the internal consultancy idea.

Step 1: Build rapport

Head of TD: 'Hello Chris how are you? How was your trip to the Isle of Wight?
Director of HR: 'Oh it was great, it was good to get the boat out and to see the family but the weather could have been better, made me realise that I should do it more often'.
Head of TD: 'Are you going again soon?'
Director of HR: 'Yes we are going to go again for the bank holiday and the weather forecast is a lot better'
Head of TD: 'Won't you miss the big match if you go then?'
Director of HR: 'No I have thought of that already. There is a club house with the sports channel and are we are inviting the boys to join us, so it should be a great

weekend, I'm really looking forward to it. What about you what about your trip to China, how did it go?'

Head of TD: 'It was brilliant, it's an amazing place, things change before your eyes. Do you know that I'm pretty sure they built a new hotel in the two weeks we were there. Oh and the food, don't get me started about the food. I didn't know whether to eat it or photograph it first.

Director of HR: 'I expect you got some great photos though.'

Head of TD: 'Yes I took masses and masses of photos, which I need to sort out. The Great Wall was spectacular.

Director of HR: 'So what have you been up to since you have come back?'

(Note how the building rapport stage seems to come to a natural end and the other party will often ask you a question that moves the conversation on to a more business footing. Resist the temptation to launch into talking about the proposal to move from stand-up training delivery to internal consultancy, and instead set the scene for why the director of HR should listen to you.)

Step 2: Establish credibility

Outline the background to your desire to influence them in a way that would be of interest and relevance to them in terms of their agenda on the organisational hierarchy.

Head of TD: 'Since I have been back I have been reflecting on how to make sure the organisation gets the most out of its investment; talking to managers about the challenges they are facing at the moment and how we can help to make them become more effective, and its been very revealing.

Director of HR: 'Oh that's interesting and what did they say?'

Head of TD: 'Well on the whole they were complimentary; they think we are doing a good job. But, they are concerned about the level of challenge they are facing over the next few months and they have a very tough agenda to achieve. They value the training department but are beginning to see releasing staff as quite a luxury and they told me that they might not be able to send the number of staff on courses this year. This is reflected in the reduction in numbers we have been seeing over the past few months.

'Interestingly I was chatting to two colleagues in other organisations about this too and they are saying similar things about attendance. Their managers are finding it difficult to release staff and are saying that they need to refocus resources on the business rather than development.

Director of HR: 'That's interesting. I have to admit I have had some similar conversations with managers myself, the feedback from your department is always good but they feel that it might be becoming a bit of a luxury these days, particularly when they are asked to demonstrate value for money all the time. It's difficult.'

Head of TD: 'Do you know we did a couple of pieces of work with the sales team earlier in the year and they are now converting 30 per cent more leads into sales. We also did a review of the performance appraisal system, found where the block was in the organisation, and now more than 90 per cent of staff have an appraisal instead of 40 per cent, which as you know, has been proven to improve staff retention and reduce recruitment costs.

Director of HR: 'Yes I heard about those initiatives, in fact a couple of managers told me that they could do with some help to look at why they have such a high staff turnover.'

Head of TD: 'I think a lot of managers are under a great deal of pressure to achieve results at the moment and there are lots of ways that we could help them to respond to the challenges they face, particularly as the opportunity to bring in external consultants has been significantly cut back. Also, I believe staff like training and development initiatives that directly impact on their ability to do their job better and get better results. Being involved in projects like this develops staff and managers too.'

Director of HR: 'Sounds to me as though you have a plan Sam...'

(Note: I hope you can see how the Head of TD was gradually building up the business case until the Director of HR was prompted to ask if there was a particular idea or request behind these comments.)

Step 3: Make your request

Head of TD: 'Yes since you mention it, I have. I think we should consider putting the bulk of our resources into working directly with managers to address their business needs rather than using the annual training needs analysis menu driven approach we use at the moment.

Director of HR: 'That's an interesting idea – how would you deal with the reaction from managers and staff that they are having something useful and valuable taken away from them?

Head of TD: 'I think we need to keep mandatory training and then use a transparent bidding process to establish which projects we are going to work on, make sure we evaluate the outcome, and promote the benefits and learning to the rest of the organisation.

Director of HR: 'I need to talk to a few more people about this but in the meantime would you produce a report for the board outlining the benefits and why you think we should go down this route for the next meeting in May?

Head of TD: 'Yes of course Chris, I would be happy to do that.'

Step 4: Follow up and thanks

Head of TD sends an email to the Director of HR following their earlier chat.

> *Hi Chris*
>
> *Just wanted to say how much I appreciated our conversation regarding improving the effectiveness of the training and development investment within the organisation, and would like to take you up on the offer to present a paper to the board in May. Thank you for giving me this opportunity. I will present an outline structure by the end of next week for your approval.*
>
> *In the meantime I hope you have a successful sailing trip over the bank holiday.*

When expressing your thanks avoid raising other issues or complications, which the other person will need to think about or act on. Just a simple thanks and a restatement of what you intend to do next is all that is required.

Please bear in mind that it might take several different conversations with several different stakeholders to influence the change in the way that development was provided within the organisation. You need to see each separate conversation as part of the process and then enable each of the people you have influenced to reflect on the idea and start talking about the idea with other people. When people start to 'join the dots up' your ideas will start to gather momentum, and if it's a good idea, people will start to persuade other people of its merits.

I recommend that you follow these steps in the order I have set out, and that you learn the skills that correspond with all of the steps.

Influencing – a personal example

I wanted to interview a chief executive officer for this book. I had heard about him through the 'grape vine' and thought that he might be working at the level of peacemaker. I needed a practical example for the chapter on making peace but I was also curious to meet him.

I am an independent consultant and I am aware that CEOs receive hundreds of unsolicited approaches from people like me every week. Over the previous two years I had coached a couple of people in this organisation. I was invited to do so by an ex client who was working there at the time.

As the saying goes 'you only have one opportunity to make a good first impression' and I really wanted to meet this man. I considered sending a copy of the People Skills Revolution, mentioning my coaching experience, asking directly for an interview and hoping for the best.

I then had a brain wave. I would contact my ex client, who is now a friend, outlining the background to the request, explain how I proposed to approach the CEO, reassure him that my interest was research rather than commerical and ask him his opinion on my strategy. I also mentioned that I was seeking other examples for the book including negotiation.

I believed that my friend had a number of options here. He could have ignored the request although I felt that was unlikely due to our long-standing friendship. He could have made comments on my approach and that would have been very helpful to me. Or he could have done something better than this, which I was totally not expecting.

Within minutes, my friend, who had now moved on to another organisation came back to me and had gained agreement for me to have a two-hour interview with the CEO.

The transcript of this conversation forms the basis of the chapter on 'making peace'. I found the interview fascinating since it tracks the CEO's personal development journey from his original decision to become more assertive through the stages of influencing, negotiation, conciliation, taking a stand, to becoming a peacemaker.

But the really interesting interaction in this scenario is the action of the ex client/friend. Not only did he go out of his way to help me by facilitating the meeting but he also had lunch with me to tell me the brilliant example of negotiation that you will find in the next chapter, which had me and him in fits of laughter.

I believe this is an example of how both parties can enjoy influencing, even when only one of them has an agenda. To close the loop I wrote a personal note to both the CEO and my friend to tell them how much I had appreciated the time and effort they had taken to help me. Later on, I also shared the draft of the chapters they had helped me with so that I could check that they were comfortable with the way I had interpreted the stories that they shared with me.

Influencing – a client's story

One of my clients was trying to build a relationship with a senior director who was notorious for being difficult to deal with. When trying to engage him in conversation she found out that he liked wine. Over a period of weeks, they bantered about which wine was best. Then one day, he brought in a bottle of wine for her to try whilst everyone else in the office looked on aghast, mouthing to each other: 'How did she do that?'

When she was telling me the story, she said that she was going to continue to disagree with him, until one day he wants to try her favourite wine. This story reflects the sense of fun that can emerge as you develop your skills to build rapport and clearly 'oils the wheels' of an improved business relationship.

Step 1: Building rapport

These days everyone is so busy that we tend to treat other people as just a 'cog in the wheel' in our projects. We are then surprised when they don't jump to our commands and deliver what we need them to deliver. The reason for this is that despite our position in the organisation, people decide to do things for people and they tend to do things for people they like. So if you want to get people to do things for you, in a timely, efficient manner, and to a high standard, you have get them on your side.

We do this very naturally with people we like but with people we don't like or don't know, it can be more difficult. Building rapport is the skill that will make the biggest difference to you in your interaction with others by increasingly your ability to walk into any situation feeling calm, confident and in control.

Before you learn to do it, you must want to do it. You have to believe that it will make a difference, appreciate the value of superficial conversation and overcome any resistance you have towards talking about subjects that you are not interested in or do not consider to be deep and meaningful.

List below five people who, at the moment, you would find it difficult to build rapport with.

1. _____

2. _____

3. _____

4, _____

5. _____

Pick three off your list to practice your building rapport skills on.

In order to build rapport effectively and find a point of connection with another person, you will need to find a genuine interest in what they are saying, understand that people communicate in different ways, develop your listening skills, and be prepared to share something about yourself.

Record any resistance you feel to building rapport with these people and examine any negative beliefs you may have by revisiting the chapter on transforming negative beliefs.

Psychological types

One of the main reasons for discomfort between two people is a lack of understanding that people communicate in different ways. We tend to get on with people who are like us, and struggle to connect with people who are very different from us. One of the best explanations of this was presented by Carl Jung in his book 'Psychological Types'[5].

In this book, which was published in 1921, Jung suggests that there are four dominant communications types, which he calls Intuitor, Thinker, Feeler and Sensor. We are all a combination of all of the types although we tend to have one or two dominant styles that determine the people we get on with easily and the people we find much harder work.

Outlined below is a grid that gives you an overview of the Intuitior, Thinker, Feeler and Sensor types, and explains their characteristics in terms of their likes, dislikes, typical occupations, their planning style, how to influence and build rapport with them.

As you read the explanations first consider what might be your dominant type or types. These are usually the ones you find yourself agreeing with as you

---

5   Princeton University Press 1976

read. The ones that you have a less positive reaction to are usually your least favoured types.

When you have done this, consider what style your boss might be, or your colleagues, your partner or your children. This will give you some clues as to how you interact with these people at the moment.

The grid below highlights the main characteristics of the four psychological types. It will also give you some idea of how to build rapport with each style and how to influence different types of people around to your point of view.

When looking at the different types it is important to remember that we are all a combination of all the styles but we have preferences that influence our behaviour.

Psychological Types

	Intuitor	Thinker	Feeler	Sensor
Orientation	**Ideas**	**Thoughts**	**Feelings**	**Actions**
Likes	Creativity Originality Sharing ideas Making plans Dreaming futures	Research Planning Organisation Review order Logic Systems Place for everything and everything in its place	Interacting with people Sharing feelings Networking Finding out about people Making judgements based on feelings/gut	Decisiveness Taking action Focusing on result
Dislikes	Routine Being bored	Clutter and chaos	Feelings not acknowledged	Too much detail People who ramble
Typical jobs	Inventors Planners Research Artists Advertising executives	Accountant Information technology Lawyer Scientist	Healthcare Sales Teaching Public relations Human resources	Engineer Production Sales executive Project manager Operations director
Planning style	Future perspective Innovation New ideas	Past, present and future perspectives Research Develop Lists Bar charts Gantt charts Project plans	Past perspective Experience Feelings Gut reactions Good or bad Judgemental	Present perspective Decide Actions that need to happen to achieve results

	Intuitor	Thinker	Feeler	Sensor
Orientation	Ideas	Thoughts	Feelings	Actions
Build rapport by	Listening to ideas Entering into their world Taking time to listen	Choose a good time Value order/ organisation Business first Keep it short Professional	Smile, pull up a chair, offer them a drink and ask them how they are	Keep it short, relevant and interesting Do it during short spaces between action
How to influence them	Get into their world. Promote newness and difference. Listen to their ideas	Give them all the facts Be prepared to answer questions Present information logically Be professional Businesslike	Take time Pull up a chair Have a chat Acknowledge feelings Emphasise human issues	Keep it short and simple Reduce long arguments into three key points Be solution focused Be prepared

Looking at the descriptions above – which of the four psychological types do you believe is your preferred style, your 'back up' style, and your least favourite style?

	Preferred style	Back up style	Least favourite style
Intuitor			
Thinker			
Feeler			
Sensor			

What style do you believe your boss, colleagues, partner or children might be?

	Preferred style
Boss	
Colleagues	
Partner	
Children	

The following grid illustrates how different styles can change their behaviour to influence other styles.

When I share this approach based on Jung's Psychological Types with people in coaching and training situations they usually ask the same question – which is: 'Does this mean that we now have to analyse all the people we come across in terms of these psychological types?'

Psychological Types Influencing Grid

	Intuitor	Thinker	Feeler	Sensor
Intuitor⟹	Share and develop ideas Be aware of 'blind spots' brought about by shared view Need to keep track of goals, budgets and deadlines	Share ideas logically Work up your idea Be prepared to talk about the past, present and the future	Present ideas in a way that is of interest or relevance to people Realise the human aspects of great ideas	Sell ideas in terms of three key benefits Test practicality before presenting ideas Make sure ideas work and are ready to go
Thinker⟹	Be ready to go into their world Recognise that they bring creativity/ difference Take time to listen before trying to focus them	Appreciate other's logic/ organisation skills Be aware of 'blind spots' brought about by shared view	Recognise need to make human issues part of the logical agenda Build in a process to involve people in planning/ decision-making	Reduce long documents and arguments into three key points that allow Sensor to make a 'yes'/'no' decision Realise they don't need all the facts

	Intuitor	Thinker	Feeler	Sensor
Feeler⇒	Be patient Take time to enable them to share their ideas Present human concerns as factors to be considered terms of impact on plans or dreams	Explain logic of human concerns Present ideas in terms of facts rather than emotion Use logic to take them from where they are to where you want them to be	Pull up a chair and have a coffee Be aware of 'blind spot' Other styles do not always explore human issues Feelings need to be explained logically not emotionally to other styles	Translate human issues into logical business benefits/ concerns Present ideas in action 'yes'/'no' terms Trade desire to be understood with ability to be heard
Sensor⇒	Be patient Take time Gradually move from general non-specific to focused and specific	Educate Thinkers to present thoughts and suggestions in three point summary form	Assist Feelers to translate emotions into logical business impacts and consequences	Just get on and do it but remember that others are not slow they are just different from you Be aware of 'blind spot'. If you want others on board you may have to slow down your drive towards actions

The answer to this question is 'no'. Most of our interactions with others are just fine and if something is working you do not need to try and fix it. Where this approach is useful is in helping you to understand those situations where you are having parallel conversations that never seem to meet or where you might even think that the person is so unlike you that you think they must come from another planet.

If you learn to adapt your style to suit the communication needs of others, you will be able to influence people around to your point of view more quickly and effectively.

Think of three people who you have some difficulty communicating with, then take a look at the descriptions.

List the person and then write down what you think their preferred way of communicating might be in terms of the Intuitor, Thinker, Feeler, Sensor model. Next, write a short statement highlighting what you could do to understand how they see the world and what you can do to get on the same wavelength with them.

1. _____

2. _____

3. _____

Now consider what communication style you should use with them to start building rapport.

Notice your reactions to the suggestion that you build rapport with them.

Building rapport for the long term

Most people like to talk about themselves, particularly if they feel that the person they are talking to is interested in what they have to say. So the answer to building rapport with these three people, and everyone else, is to be able to understand their style and then find topics of conversation that they like to engage in. Most of us have 'pet' topics that we like to talk about, although we often do not start talking about those subjects unless someone shows a degree of curiosity in us and our interests.

Your aim should be to build rapport for the long term, which means finding out about their interests and building on your knowledge of them each time you meet them. In the short term you just want to signal a readiness to engage. People that are really good at building rapport suggest that it's just about asking the other person questions about themselves to show an interest and hope that one of them touches the seam of passion that nearly all of us have.

In the first instance, this is mostly about showing a readiness to engage, so find something that you can use to start the conversation. Typical openings might include commenting on an item of clothing, noticing an unusual or interesting object or picture on their desk, or in the immediate environment, which reflects their outside interests. Then you can move on to some superficial questions that shows you are interested in them and ready to talk.

Superficial conversation is a great leveler. If you learn this skill and none of the others in this book you will feel confident to walk into a room and start a conversation with just about anyone, regardless of their seniority in the organisation or group. I have found that many people do not like superficial conversation or building rapport because they believe it's ingenuous, particularly if they are not interested in what the other person has to say. If this is true for you, you need to overcome this belief.

One way to do this is to become interested in the process of getting people to talk, rather than the content, so that every time you get someone to engage in superficial conversation, you regard it as a success. After a while you will begin to enjoy using this skill and do it quite naturally without having to think about it. In doing this, you are also likely to become much more interested in people and what they have to say.

Planning a 'building rapport conversation'

Taking the five people that you highlighted on page 79, think of at least three comments you could make, or questions you could ask, to start building rapport with them. Typical questions might be about the weekend, journeys, holidays, family, weather, hobbies and interests.

Person   Possible questions or comments

1. _____   _____

2. _____   _____

3. _____   _____

4. _____   _____

5. _____   _____

See this as a long-term goal, and build on what you have learnt about the person each time you meet them. In the first instance, they may be suspicious of your motives, which is understandable, especially if you have not got on well in the past. You will find that over time, your relationship with them will improve greatly and that your ability to influence them will increase significantly.

Building rapport can take five minutes with someone who is similar to you and has similar interests to you, but take months for someone who is antagonist or very different from you. You have to learn to pace your requests according to the level of the relationship that you have.

Once you are confident that you have built rapport with a person you want to influence and the conversation is going well, they may then say something like: 'You haven't just come here to talk about my golfing holiday, what do you want?'

When asked such a direct question as this, it is very tempting to just make your request. Try to resist doing this until you have taken the time to establish your credibility (or why they should listen to you) with them.

Step 2: Establishing credibility

Establishing your credibility or indicating why other people should listen to you involves calmly and assertively outlining aspects of you, your experience and your background, which might be of interest and relevance to them. For a lot of people, the very thought of doing this takes them way out of their comfort zone, but it is also the difference between getting yourself heard and getting your ideas and requests overlooked.

One of the reasons I think people feel uncomfortable with establishing credibility is that they fear that they will come across as arrogant since that's how they perceive the people who do it. This is not about making claims about yourself that are not true or inflated in an aggressive manner.

Rather it is simply about sharing information about yourself that would be relevant to the other person and the situation you are raising with them. A friend who had been practising these techniques said it was about finding a way to do this with subtlety, and I completely agree with this. To start with, you might feel that you are coming across like a 'bull in a china shop' but as you relax into it, you will learn what information to share, with whom, and when would be the most appropriate time to do this.

The most simple way to establish your credibility is to get reacquainted with your sources of power. There are lots of categories for power but here are the ones I find most useful:

- **Legitimate** from your authority or role.
- **Referent** from your personality.
- **Information** from your knowledge base.
- **Expertise** from your background and experience.
- **Reward** from what you can offer to people in relation to their needs.
- **Coercive** from you ability to make others do things they don't want to do.

Planning to establish your credibility

We all have these sources of power, although we tend to forget we have them. Jot down some notes against each of these headings and keep coming back to them until you think you have a complete and clear picture of your background, knowledge, skills, personal qualities, temperament and experience.

A good clue to your areas of expertise is to think of the times when people come to you for advice, rather than going to a colleague. An indication of your reward power is what you can do for people when they have done an especially good job for you, for example putting them on a course that might be beneficial to them or giving them a particular task that you know they will enjoy.

Although I would not suggest that you get good at using your coercive power, it is important to realise that you do have it and that it can be used appropriately when necessary, for example, to call security if a situation gets out of hand or to use company policies and procedures where necessary.

How would you demonstrate that you have these sources of power?

Legitimate:

Referent:

Information:

Expertise:

Reward:

Coercive:

Although I have found that most people feel highly uncomfortable doing this exercise and then taking action to try it out, if you want to influence someone around to your point of view, you have to establish your credibility with them first.

Once you have highlighted your sources of power, practise talking about them out loud to yourself, or start slipping some establishing credibility comments into a normal work or social conversation and notice the impact that they have. The more you do this the more comfortable you will become with the skill until you find yourself doing it without even thinking about it.

Taking action – building rapport and establishing your credibility

Now thinking about the five people you wanted to build rapport with, how would you adapt what you have written above to be of interest and relevance to them in order to influence them?

What might the five target people want or be interested to know about you in order to listen to you?

Target person	Information of relevance and interest to them
1. _____	_____
2. _____	_____
3. _____	_____
4. _____	_____
5. _____	_____

DO IT!
Report back

What actions did you take to practise establishing your credibility?

What reaction did you get?

How did it make you feel?

What would you do differently next time?

The hierarchy of language

Another element to consider when learning to influence, is to understand that language has a hierarchy, particularly in the business world. Your agendas will not be the same as others on different stages on the organisational structure. In the same way that Jung's psychological types suggests that you adapt your style so that other styles can hear and understand what you are saying, the hierarchy of language encourages you to slant your needs to be of relevance to the needs and agendas of the people at other levels in the organisation. I have simplified these levels as on the shop floor, supervisor, manager, strategist and consultant, who hovers towards the top of the organisational structure without being formally part of it.

The Hierarchy of Language

Agendas at each level of the hierarchy

If you are working directly with clients 'on the shop floor', your concerns will be:

- the quality of the service you are providing,
- the resources you have available to you,
- any operational issues and difficulties,
- getting the job done and doing it well,
- your own personal safety and the safety of the people you work with and for.

If you are a supervisor, your major concerns will be:

- achieving targets and deadlines,
- getting the goods out of the door,

- minimising complaints,
- working within available resources,
- finding solutions to problems,
- achieving safe working practices.

If you are a manager, your concerns and agenda shift again. They will be:

- introducing change,
- concern for the customers as a group,
- improving systems and procedures,
- limiting expenditure and reducing cost,
- implementing strategic initiatives,
- advocating a case for additional resources,
- developing health and safety policies and procedures.

If you are a strategist, your agendas and concerns will be:

- competition with other similar organisations,
- managing the relationship with shareholders and internal/external stakeholders,
- meeting financial performance targets to increase profit or stay within budget,
- establishing organisational goals/targets,
- projecting a positive image of the organisation,
- corporate responsibility for health and safety.

This strategist agenda explains why you could be working in an organisation that you may consider to be poorly run and inefficient, but when you read the press releases, it paints a wonderfully positive image. This is the nature of the role. If you want to influence a strategist, tell them something that would help them to improve the promotion of the service or business, or help them to avoid receiving criticism from stakeholders and shareholders.

If there are senior people within the organisation who are not part of the management structure, for example consultants on a major project or in a healthcare setting, this group will also have their own language agendas.

The agendas of the consultant will be:

- influencing the management structure,
- the quality of the service,
- sufficiency of resources,
- their status in relation to others,
- their self-image,
- hidden agendas,
- safety of procedures.

A member of staff was heard complaining to a secretary that she had not been able to get a consultant to engage with her project. The secretary kept on typing, turned her head and said matter of factly: 'Have you tried flattery?' While you may recoil at the thought of using flattery to get your ideas considered, would you rather be heard or ignored?

The way to use these agendas at each level of the organisation is to realise that if you present your arguments in the language of their interests rather than your own, you will substantially increase your chances of getting your views accepted. This is not an easy skill to learn, but once you develop this technique, your influencing skills will be enhanced significantly.

Translating your agendas into other agendas in the hierarchy

Imagine the head of training and development mentioned on page 73 wanted to sell the idea of moving to a more consultancy role throughout the organisation. The example below provides some suggestions for selling the idea into their agenda at the shop floor, supervisor, manager, strategist and consultant level.

Head of training and development to people on the shop floor level

You know that their agendas include quality of service, resources available, operational issues and difficulties, getting the job done and doing it well.

'I would like the training department to do more consultancy work rather than stand-up training'.

You might want to do this because:

- you feel that too many of the people who are coming on courses either don't need the training or are not interested to learn,
- your course participants are increasingly saying that they are too busy to attend your courses,
- some areas have chronic problems and these are not addressed,
- a number of managers have requested more specific training for their team and are less satisfied with 'off the shelf' solutions,
- you are undertaking a professional development course and know you could assist the departments more and are frustrated that your skills are not being used.

Head of training and development to people on the supervisor level

You know that their agendas include concerns for achieving targets and deadlines, minimising complaints, finding solutions to problems and achieving safe working.

'I would like the training department to do more consultancy work rather than stand-up training.'

You might want to do it because it would:

- increase the ability to tailor each initiative to specific business problems,
- provide the ability to talk to manager's about their needs and design something specifically for them,
- enable us to react more quickly and flexibly to identified needs,
- make us more customer focused and led,
- provide opportunity to evaluate the benefits to the business more closely,
- raise profile of department when we demonstrate the benefits of consultancy projects we have done,
- reduce cost of bringing in external consultants,
- reactions to the approach could be managed by maintaining mandatory training and establishing a process to keep in greater contact with the managers.

Head of training and development to people on the manager level

You know that their agendas include introducing change, concern for customers as a group, improving systems and procedures, implementing strategic initiatives.

'I would like the training department to do more consultancy work rather than stand-up training.'

You might want to do it because it would:

- be in line with what other organisations are doing,
- address feedback from managers that they are looking for development for their staff with more flexibility,
- provide research data on how consultancy can be evaluated more easily than training delivery,
- illustrate that consultancy can be more cost-effective than adopting a 'scatter gun' approach to training.

Head of training and development to people on the strategist level

You know that their agendas include concerns for competition with other, similar organisations, managing the relationship with shareholders and stakeholders, meeting financial perfomance targets, projecting a positive image of the organisation and increasing profit.

'I would like the training department to do more consultancy work rather than stand-up training.'

You might want to do it because it would:

- be a strategic initiative supported by relevant professional organisations,
- make the organisation leaner and more productive,
- you will be able to quantify anticipated cost savings,
- it has been successful in this and other, similar organisations,
- respond to request form a significant number of managers,
- make the organisation sound interesting, innovative and exciting.

Head of training and development to people on the consultant level

Consultants are people who operate towards the top of the hierarchy but are not usually part of the management structure. You know that their agendas include concerns to improve their status, self-image, hidden agendas and quality of the service.

'I would like the training department to do more consultancy work rather than stand-up training.'

You might want to do it because it would:

- provide them useful with experiences that will give them the edge when taking on other projects,
- (if it is safe to do so) explain how you are influencing people and invite them to be part of the process,
- (by asking their advice on your approach) invite them to comment and make suggestions on your influencing strategy.

I hope you can see that the shifts in language to address the different agendas are subtle, but they are present. You will become much more effective when influencing others when you sell your ideas into their agendas rather than your own.

Allow the people you are trying to influence to get some kudos at the level they are working at without having to do much of the work or the thinking.

One way to do this is to imagine them selling your idea upwards to their boss or stakeholders. You can do this by looking at their upwards agendas and including the attraction of your idea to their boss, into your establishing credibility at Step 2 of the influencing cycle.

In order to influence you must let go of an initiative being your idea and gain satisfaction from the fact that when someone does something that you influenced them to do, that you played a large part in achieving that goal. In fact the more you can step back from the outcome the more successful you will become as an influencer.

Taking action – planning to influence upwards, downwards and across

Think of something you would like to influence within your organisation or group.

What is it?

What are your concerns and agendas in relation to this change?

How would you sell your idea downwards or across to people on the shop floor?

How would you sell your idea upwards or across to a supervisor?

How would you sell your idea upwards or across to a manager?

How would you sell your idea upwards or across to a strategist?

How would you sell your idea upwards or across to a consultant working towards the top of the organisational hierarchy, but who is not formally part of the management structure?

What is stopping you having these conversations?

When can you hold these conversations with people?

DO IT!
Report back

What happened when you talked to people about your influencing idea in terms of their own agendas?

What went well?

What would you do differently next time?

The answers to these questions, added to your knowledge of their psychological types, and an understanding of your sources of power, should assist you to take action to build rapport and establish credibility with the person you want to influence.

Once you have built rapport and established your credibility with the people you want to influence, either an opening will naturally appear in the conversation for you to ask for what you want – they may even ask you directly why you want to speak to them – or you will have to identify an opportunity to make your request.

Before making your request you need to be absolutely clear about what you want to get out of the influencing interaction. You are now ready to move on to Step 3 of the model, which is to 'make your request'.

Step 3: Make your request

Most people are averse to taking on extra work, so try to make your suggestion attractive to them and easy for them to say 'yes' to with very little additional work on their part. So when people ask you 'what do you want to happen?', make your request in a clear and concise manner that will encourage them to move towards a 'yes'.

With the idea you want to influence firmly in your mind, if you were asked the direct question 'what would you want to happen?', what would you say?

Make sure you are clear and have prepared as much of the ground as possible to make it easy for the other person to say 'yes' to your request.

For larger projects, rather than focus on just one person to influence, include a number of people in your strategy and chat to people about your ideas with a 'light touch', presenting your idea in a way that suits their psychological type, interest in the topic, and level in organisational hierarchy. You will find that providing your approach is logical and has clear business benefits, people will start talking about your idea, 'joining up the dots', putting your idea on the agenda. The decision to go ahead will fall naturally out of those discussions.

Step 4: Follow up and thanks

We are all very busy these days, and going out of our way to do things for people takes additional time and effort. If someone successfully influences someone to do something for them and they take action on their behalf to pursue a goal, it is polite and advisable to thank them for doing so. Without this very simple step, it will be more difficult to build rapport with the person the next time you meet and it will be harder to establish credibility and make a request. Saying thanks or providing information or support, which might be useful to the other person, is respectful and creates an economy of thanks, which can become part of the culture of an organisation and 'how we work around here'.

What can you do or say to express your appreciation of the time they have spent with you or any actions that other people have taken on your behalf?

Be careful to make your thank you message short and simple so that the other person can see at a glance that it is a note of appreciation or thanks. Do not use Step 4 as an opportunity to ask for something else from them.

The power of chats

I am a huge fan of 'chats'. This book would not have been written without being able to chat to my clients, colleagues and friends, who listened to my thoughts, helped me to shape my ideas and gave me feedback on the initial draft. I have also realised over the years that being able to hold a conversation is a lot less common that you imagine. I remember working with one coaching client over a number of weeks, when he turned to me and said: 'Are we having a conversation? Is this what having a conversation feels like?' It was at this point that I realised that something I take completely for granted and sustains me intellectually and emotionally may not be something that other people benefit from in a routine way.

When working with my clients and assisting them to develop their skills, it is not long before I encourage them to embrace the power of chats. I suggest that they find people they connect with (regardless of organisational structures or professions) who they enjoy talking to and who can spare the time to chat to them about things of mutual interest.

Although initially they find the concept a bit strange, once they get going and form relationships that they value, they are constantly on the look out for people who they can trust to act as their 'sounding boards'.

I have been chatting professionally for over 12 years. I now believe that other people often have the missing pieces to your puzzles and in the course of your conversation they will say something that will become an 'aha' moment for you. These chats develop your thoughts further, tell you who to speak to next or what books to read to deepen your expertise. It often feels that the people I chat to have a message for me just waiting to be collected, and the more conversations like this I have the more of these magic moments I seem to receive.

It is important when embracing the power of chats, not to have preconceived ideas about what will come out of the discussions. Rather you should just allow the conversation to flow naturally, sharing your ideas, thoughts, feelings and actions. When you are both energised by the talk that bounces between you, the sparks of inspiration will fly 'thick and fast'.

These conversations do not have to be formal meetings. They can be held over a coffee, during lunch, by the water cooler or in the corridor.

Make a list of five people who you have met briefly and feel that you might be able to have an interesting chat with.

1. _____

2. _____

3. _____

4. _____

5. _____

DO IT!
Taking action – the power of chats

How could you suggest to these people that you met for a chat?

What is stopping you from having this conversation?

What can you do to overcome your resistance?

When are you going to meet at least one of these people for a conversation?

Report back

When did you have this conversation?

What happened?

What new insights or suggestions did you receive?

What would you do differently next time?

How would you build on this success?

How to become a better listener

In the People Skills Revolution, I refer to a four-stage model of listening presented by Julie Starr in the 'Coaching Manual'[6], which I have found very useful when talking to clients about developing their listening skills.

I have worked with work teams and departments who have reported a dramatic improvement in communication just by making a very simple shift in where they were placing their attention when listening to their colleagues and clients.

---

6   Prentice Hall Business 2010

Hierarchy of Listening

It looks as though I am listening but I'm not really

I am engaged in the conversation, but I am looking for an opportunity to say what I want to say next.

I am focusing my attention on you, I am listening for details, facts, patterns

I am picking up things you are saying and things you are not saying, I am getting a sense of who you are

What this approach demonstrates very clearly is that the level at which we listen to people is a choice we make based on our skills and our interest in the other person. We can make the decision to improve our ability to listen by moving from cosmetic or conversational listening to focus our attention on the other person in a deliberate and conscious manner. The moment we actively listen, the information that we will pick up about the person will significantly increase.

Once you become skilled in active listening you will find that almost without trying you will start to pick up information from the other person that they do not realise they are giving. This level is called deep listening and can only be accessed by developing your active listening skills. As an executive coach, this is where I like to operate when I am given the opportunity. When you reach this level you will find that you are tuning in and out of the conversation and you are looking at the person in a slightly different way. I believe that I do my best work when I operate at the deep listening level. I also believe that more often that not, if I listen closely, the other person will give me the answers to the dilemmas they are facing. Then I simply have to reflect their thoughts back to them.

Taking action – how to become a better listener

Developing your listening skills

Identify where on the hierarchy of listening you tend to operate

Are there some people you find it particularly difficult to 'tune into'? Why is this?

List three situations where you could develop your listening skills further.

1. _____

2. _____

3. _____

What actions can you take to practice moving from a cosmetic or conversational listening style to an active listening style?

A key skill in listening is to pull out the main patterns and themes rather than concentrate on the detail of what people are saying. What would help you to listen for these patterns and themes?

When could you try out listening at a different level?

DO IT!
Report back

What happened?

What patterns and themes did you identify in the course of your listening?

What went well?

What would you do differently next time?

How to become a better questioner

I once asked a woman who was incredibly popular and highly skilled at building rapport, how she achieved that. She said: 'You just keep asking them questions about themselves, and if you are lucky they will ask you something back.'

Unfortunately today we are generally quite suspicious of people who show an interest in us, and want to know what their motives are. So in order to become a better questioner I suggest you follow the following guidelines.

Guidelines for becoming a better questioner:

- Show genuine interest.
- Don't expect reciprocity.
- Ask questions until you hit a seam of enthusiasm.
- Know when to back off when the other person doesn't want to engage.
- Adopt a relaxed, curious and interested style.
- Be clear about the intentions behind your questions.
- Realise that when people genuinely feel you are interested in them, they like to answer questions about themselves, because they like the attention.
- Repeat questions in a different way to demonstrate real interest.
- Pay attention to the style and chemistry of both parties.
- Use probing questions sensitively and persistently to enable personal awareness.
- Respect confidentiality.
- Experiment when people respond with 'I don't know' answers by posing the question 'and if you did know, what would you say? '

Taking action – how to become a better questioner

Think of someone you find it difficult to establish a point of connection with. What do you know about that person in terms of their social life, interests, enthusiasms and family?

What could you say to begin a conversation with them that is not directly about work?

What questions could you ask them about themselves?

What would your intention behind asking these questions be?

What is stopping you from doing this?

How can you overcome these barriers?

What would be the best environment to start building rapport with them and to find something out about them?

When could you try to engage them in conversation?

DO IT!
Report back

What happened when you used your building rapport, listening and questioning skills to engage this person in conversation?

How can you build on this outcome in the future?

Influencing – planning an influencing conversation

Think of someone you would like to influence.

What would you like to influence them about and why?

Step 1: Build rapport

What do you know about them that would assist you to build rapport with them?

What would you say is their dominant psychological type: Intuitor, Thinker, Feeler, Sensor?

How will their psychological type affect the way in which you build rapport and establish your credibility with them?

What questions or observations could you make to initiate a conversation with them?

What would you be prepared to share about yourself in terms of your interests, enthusiasms, hobbies, family and amusing stories in order to make the building rapport process balanced?

Step 2: Establish your credibility

Where are they on the organisational hierarchy?

What are their interests and concerns on the hierarchy of language?

Looking at the types of power exercise you completed on page 88, what legitimate, referent, information, expert, reward and coecive power do you have that would be of interest and relevance to this person and encourage them to listen to you?

Combining these factors together, write yourself a script, outlining how you would establish your credibility with this person. Most people who aren't doing this already baulk at the prospect of doing this exercise because they don't like 'blowing their own trumpet' and feel it takes them way of out their comfort zone.

If you want to achieve the benefits of influencing and all the more sophisticated skills that build on becoming more assertive, you need to overcome this feeling. Claim your skills, knowledge and experience by demonstrating in a simple, subtle and positive way, why they should listen to you. The more you do this and achieve improved reactions from others, the more natural it will begin to feel.

What is your establishing credibility script (or why they should listen to you) for this person?

Step 3: Make your request

Imagine that you have successfully established your credibility and you have been invited to say what you want to happen. What would you say to clearly and explicitly make your request. Phrase your statement in such a way that the most obvious reaction to your intervention is 'yes'

Step 4: Follow up and thanks

What could you do or say to show your appreciation of the time they have taken to listen to your proposal. How would you acknowledge the genuine contributions they have made in helping you to achieve your goals?

Taking action – influencing

When would you be able to have this conversation?

What actions do you have to take to make this conversation happen?

What is stopping you from having this conversation?

What can you do to overcome your resistance?

DO IT!
Report back

What happened when you had the conversation with the person you wanted to influence?

What went well?

What did not go well?

What would you do next time to build on all the things that went well?

Reflection: We have covered a lot of ground in this section. What successes have you achieved?

What skills do you still need to practice to become more natural in your approach?

What resistance did you feel to using the techniques outlined in this chapter and what did you do to overcome this resistance?

Remember: The ability to influence is a skill, which will get better over time. Having used this approach for many years I find that after going around the cycle of influence several times, people often initiate assistance and action that is beneficial to me without having to make a request, and as a result, working life becomes a much more enjoyable experience.

There is a lot to remember when you start to influence. It could feel very mechanical to you. It might also come across as not very natural to the person you are talking to. One way to get over this is to practice the elements individually and begin to develop your own style, which you are comfortable with. If you keep going, the pieces of the puzzle will begin to slot into place as you build one success onto another.

If there are no clear business benefits but you are still ploughing on with your agenda, it is possible that you are trying to manipulate people around to your point of view.

Whilst assertiveness builds the foundations for our people skills, Influencing starts to create the building blocks to enable us to achieve our goals and dreams. Although there is a lot to learn, if you start to practise the techniques, after a while you will start to do them naturally. You will know when you are succeeding, not just because you are getting your suggestions heard and adopted, but also because people will spontaneously start doing things for you without you even asking. They will do this because you have taken the time to get to know them and are able to present your ideas in a way that makes sense to them. They will also have got to know something of you as a person and recognise that you are a reliable and professional person to do business with.

Once you have learnt to influence and gained a number of successes in your dealings with others, you will become curious about what else you can achieve through people skills. The next level of skills up the continuum of interpersonal skills is negotiation.

Negotiation

In influencing you are asking someone to do something for you, which suits your agenda. You do this by illustrating how your agenda might be of benefit to them. In negotiation you have your agenda but so does the other party. You have wants and needs and they have wants and needs. In negotiation the art is to slowly reveal your agenda whilst gradually identifying theirs. The successful negotiation will take place in the overlap between what they want and what you want. Ideally it will be right in the middle so that both parties believe that they have achieved a winning agreement.

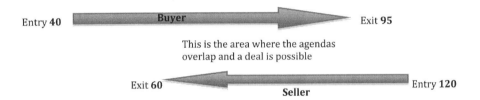

Having run many negotiation workshops in the past, it is clear to me that the best negotiators have the firmness that assertiveness provides, combined with the ability to influence others using a relaxed and confident style. What is added at this level of the continuum of interpersonal skills is persuasion, clarity as to where you are in the process at any given time, and being able to read the reactions of the other party, adjusting your approach as the negotiation progresses.

Effective negotiators also have another quality, which sets them apart from other people. They see negotiation opportunities everywhere and they believe that they can achieve successful results using their people skills. They also very much enjoy the process and can spot other negotiators and look forward to playing the negotiation game with them. This is true even when the stakes are high and the factors are very complex.

Many people at the cusp of influencing and negotiation have told me that it is their lack of self-belief that holds them back. They believe they are not good at it, they don't spot the opportunities, they don't feel they know what they are doing, they don't feel they know the right time to cut the deal, they feel that others have got the better of them and feel that they should share less information.

Before you start to develop your negotiation skills, you need to believe that a win-win solution is possible and then use a structured, step-by-step approach to gradually lead you through the process towards a successful outcome.

What is your experience of negotiation?

What did you feel about the outcomes you achieved and why?

When was the last time you spotted a negotiation opportunity?

What did you do about it?

How would you describe your approach to negotiation?

What would make you more enthusiastic and optimist about your ability to negotiate?

As people move up the continuum of interpersonal skills the need to have a structured approach increases. This enables you to clarify the agenda, avoid conflict from arising, and gradually funnel the issues down to a successful conclusion.

When I negotiate and train people in negotiation skills, I use a four-step model, which has been adapted from 'Perfect Negotiation' by Gavin Kennedy[7], who is a world leader in negotiation education.

A Step by Step Approach
Negotiation

**Step 1
Prepare**
Know your aims

**Step 2
Debate**
Reveal the agendas

**Step 3
Propose**
What you will trade for what you want?

**Step 4
Bargain**
Tease out details of agreement

---

7   Random House Business 2003

■ **Step 1:** Prepare – know your aims and what you want to achieve
■ **Step 2:** Debate – both parties gradually reveal their agendas
■ **Step 3:** Propose – identify what will you trade in return for what you want
■ **Step 4:** Bargain – tease out the details of your agreement

In order to demonstrate this set of skills in a practical way, I asked one of my previous coaching clients, who is an expert negotiator, if he could give me an example that would demonstrate the negotiation process clearly. I am very grateful to him for sharing the following scenario with me and for allowing me to share it in this handbook.

Negotiation – a practical example

The background to this negotiation is that he was the director of finance in a large hospital trust where one of its hospitals had been funded by a Private Finance Initiative or PFI. He was approached by one of the investing partners, who we will call the Bank of Non Europe, to provide a signature that would allow them to sell off their interest in the PFI. At this point he got of flash of intuition, which said: 'Why should I sign it?' Spotting a negotiation opportunity the director of finance opened up the discussions with them.

As well as a skilled negotiator he is also an avid chess player and, as I describe the events as they unfolded, I hope you can see the similarity between playing chess and the negotiation process.

Here is how the process unravelled.

Step 1: Preparation

The director of finance was aware of the following information as he went into the negotiation process.

■ The bank could have sold their interest in the PFI, without the need for a signature from the trust, in 18 months' time, suggesting a sense of urgency to sell it now.

- The trust head office was very conservative and would regard it as a risk to sign the document and would need to be convinced that it was safe and advisable to do this.
- He found out that two other trusts had agreed to sign the document for a fee of £25k.
- The representatives from the bank said that the company wanted to pull all their investments out of Europe.
- The bank agreed to pay the out-of-pocket expenses to complete the deal.
- The director of finance had no incentive to do the deal apart from the possibility of attracting funds to a trust, which was strapped for cash.
- The PFI was governed by a Department of Health national contract, which the bank was bound by.
- He enjoyed negotiation and sensed that it might be enjoyable to do business with the bank executives.

During the process of the negotiation, a friend of the director of finance, who worked in the banking industry, suggested he look at the current dollar exchange rate as a significant factor in the desire to do a deal sooner rather than later.

Step 2: Debate

The debate step allowed the director of finance to build rapport with the company executives whilst at the same time uncovering their agenda and gradually revealing his.

In opening he told the executives: 'I like you guys and I feel I know a lot about your country since I watched an iconic, popular TV programme as a kid.'

They were highly complimentary to him and graciously offered him the £25k that he was aware had been paid to the other two trusts. This was the bank's entry point.

He then said that he would sign the contract for one million. This was the director of finance's entry point.

They replied by saying that there was 'no way' they were paying that. The director of finance responded by indicating that he had no need to sign the document and said he hoped that they enjoyed their extra year and a half in Europe.

Since they had not offered to pay him more than £25k, he was prepared to walk away. This was his exit point.

A few weeks later the bank came back and had paid a lawyer to look at the contract and said that they had found a way around needing his signature.

The director of finance responded by saying that because of the Freedom of Information Act, he would be duty bound to disclose how the bank had 'stuffed' an NHS trust.

The bank executives then suggested that his request might fall under the Bribery Act. In response, the director of finance stated that the money would be going to the trust and not to him personally.

It was also clear that the Department of Health was distancing itself from the issue and was therefore not going to be a significant factor in the negotiation as it was progressing.

The bank executives also stated that they were under considerable pressure from their outside Europe head office to do the deal. The director of finance reassuringly offered to talk directly to the people who were putting pressure on them. When they pointed out the time difference, he said that to help them out he would be prepared to take a call from them at any time of the day or night.

Two senior London-based bank executives then travelled to the trust premises to find out what he would be prepared to accept.

Step 3: Propose

During the meeting at the trust headquarters, in the presence of a witness, the director of finance requested a 'significant six figure sum', if he was to agree to sign the document on behalf of the NHS trust.

The executives returned to London and the next morning, sent an email offering 100,000 dollars, which at the, then, current exchange rate was about £60,000.

At this point the banking friend reminded the director that if the bank executives did not do a deal now, they would stand to lose a fortune on the exchange rates if they had to wait 18 months to sell their investments.

The director of finance responded by saying that the trust did not deal in dollars and he reminded them that he had asked for a significant six figure amount.

Step 4: Bargain

Having established his credibility as an effective negotiator, the bank executives then asked him directly what he would accept and he told them that his signature would cost them £175K. The Bank agreed to pay the trust this amount.

Due to the length of time, effort and resources the bank was prepared to dedicate to this negotiation, one can only conclude that they, as well as the trust, were satisfied with the outcome.

When I asked the director of finance what he thought their agenda was, and what his agenda was, this is what he said.

1. The bank's agenda

It was clear that the bank wanted to get the maximum out of their investment and that the longer they held their part of the PFI the worse off they were.

They let me know what pressure they were under as individuals.

The bribery statements reflected their sense of desperation.

I left them alone – they came to me and went out of their way to do a deal with me.

They tried to make me feel unreasonable by saying that other trusts had signed the document.

I then asked him what he thought his own agenda was:

2. The director of finance agenda

Although the board was conservative, I managed to get permission from the trust to do anything I wanted to do.

It was clear that Department of Health was not going to intervene.

I also talked about the pressure I was under from a very conservative board.

I pointed out the potential consequences of doing a legal dodge to avoid having to obtain a signature from me.

I put them under psychological pressure by picking a big random number of one million as an entry point strategy.

I built empathy with them by agreeing that it was difficult to be put under pressure from head office and by making 'tongue in cheek' comments about knowing their country through the iconic children's programme I watched as a child.

To enjoy the process, and to more than cover my salary, so that I was able to say 'you have got me for free this year'.

The director of finance told me he knew that both parties were aware that it was a game and that both sides were happy with the outcome.

He also mentioned that it was an entertaining sideline to keep him, the office and his family amused whilst he got on with the real business of 'balancing the books' in a financially challenged organisation.

This example demonstrates that the essence of negotiation is that it should be a meeting of two equal minds, where both parties can spot the opportunities, avoid being deflected, and keep following a process until they gradually identify the overlap to reach a bargain.

Planning a negotiation conversation

To become an effective negotiator you must start to spot opportunities and look for the possibility of 'doing a deal' in virtually every buyer/seller scenario. If you adopt this stance you can always decide against trying to negotiate after reading the signals from the other party.

Negotiating on fairly low value and low risk situations will give you the confidence and experience to approach the more difficult and complex negotiation games.

Over the past few months, what opportunities to negotiate have you spotted?

What negotiation opportunities do you think you might have missed?

What negotiation opportunities might exist over the next three months, for example agreeing a work contract, achieving a higher salary, buying a car, or changing the balance of housework with your partner? Try to include real challenges rather than theoretical ones.

Then taking one of these scenarios, consider how you would prepare for this negotiation.

Step 1: Prepare

In the People Skills Revolution I suggest you use a preparation grid to help you identify your wants, then put a relative value on those wants in terms of importance. At the same time, you should work out your entry and exit points in relation to each of these identified wants.

To illustrate this idea, I have completed a preparation grid for the PFI signature scenario above.

Negotiation issues	Wants	Relative importance	Range entry point	Range exit point
To achieve a good deal for the trust	Use skills to achieve impressive outcome and convince conservative HQ to go ahead	Very high	Show that public sector can stand up for itself	Walk away if they don't engage
To contribute to his salary	To show the fun side of negotiation and inspire others to try	Medium	£1 million	£25k plus
To be compliant with regulations	To be transparent in negotiation process	Very high	Play game in most open way possible	Leave if accused of attempting to bribe
To enjoy the process	An amusing sideline to entertain the 'troops' with	Low	Adopt a relaxed and jovial demeanour	Decide not to play game if they would not engage with him

Now considering a negotiation you have either done in the past (and would have liked to improve) or one that you would like to do in the future; use the questions to prepare for the negotiation.

What is the negotiation worth to you?

What factors should be on your wants list?

Where can you obtain all the facts you need?

Who else do you need to talk to?

What calculations do you need to make in actual numbers and percentages?

What are your entry and exit points?

What outcomes have others achieved in a similar situation?

Then use the preparation grid below to condense your thoughts into the key issues involved in the negotiation.

Negotiation issues	Wants	Relative importance	Range entry point	Range exit point

Once you have completed your preparation you are ready to move on to Step two – debate.

Step 2: Debate

In this stage your aim is to agree the process the negotiation will follow, build rapport, reveal your agenda and identify the other party's agenda.

In the People Skills Revolution, I include a checklist of issues to consider at the debate stage to ensure that the negotiation flows smoothly. I have used the director of finance example above to show how this checklist works in practice.

The debate stage checklist

Elements	Comments
Build rapport	Talked about childhood experiences of watching iconic programme from their country. Made 'tongue in cheek' comments like 'I like you guys' and 'I hope you enjoy your extra year and a half in Europe
Set and agree agenda	It was clear that both parties had considerable experience in negotiation. As a result they kept the conversations vague to start with as they gradually revealed each other's agendas during the debate stage, and then clearly moved on to propose and bargain. For less experienced negotiators, it might be useful to be more explicit about the stages to make sure you don't jump ahead of yourself.
Describe what you are seeking	The director of finance made it clear that he wanted a completely above-board agreement, which was acceptable to his conservative head office as well as the Department of Health. He suggested he was prepared to walk away if this could not be achieved. He also clearly signalled that he wanted a substantial six figure sum and to enjoy the process.
Listen and question	He listened to the representatives of the bank and questioned them when they said they were under pressure to achieve an agreement. He also listened to his banking friend who mentioned about the exchange rate for the dollar. He also talked to the Department of Health about the discussions and found out that they were not going to intervene.

Elements	Comments
Identify available incentives or threats to facilitate movement	He was aware that the biggest risk to the bank was his ability to walk away. He also mentioned to them that if they tried to circumvent the legal requirement to get a signature, under the Freedom of Information Act, he would have no option but to release the details to the press should they ask for them (which he felt they might). This could reflect badly on the bank.
Look for signals	They told him they were under a lot of pressure from head office to achieve a deal and had gone to a lot of expense and effort to engage lawyers to find a way around the problem. They were also sending in very senior bank executives, which suggested that this was a big issue to them involving a lot of money. These signals made him much more ready to 'push his luck' in the negotiation.
Respond to signals	When they said they were under pressure from head office overseas he offered to help them out by dealing with them directly, despite the inconvenience of the time difference. When they asked him what he wanted, he stated that he wanted a significant six figure sum. When they offered him 100k dollars he responded by saying the organisation did not operate in dollars. He continually responded to their offers without dismissing them and indicating what he would prefer to happen instead.
Respond to deflections	The main attempts to deflect in this scenario were the statements that other trusts had accepted their offers, that he was attempting to bribe the bank, and that he was personally putting them in a difficult position. At each point he did not allow these suggestions to deflect him from getting a good deal for the trust, or being prepared to walk away from the negotiation if this was not achieved.
Read the energy put into the discussions by the other party	It was clear from the amount of effort they were putting into this negotiation by instructing lawyers, keeping in constant touch, and sending two bank executives to talk to him on his premises that they were extremely keen to do a deal. His signature would enable the bank to realise a lot of profit from the sale of their investments at the most opportune time.

Elements	Comments
Take a break	There were a lot of breaks in this negotiation where both parties went away to think about it, consult experts and decide the next move in the game. However neither side lost sight of the goal or the underlying process.

Use the checklist below to plan your own negotiation.

What is the negotiation?	
What are you hoping to achieve? What is it worth to you?	
How will you build rapport?	
What could you say to set and agree the agenda?	
What could you say to vaguely describe what you are seeking?	
What questions would you need to ask to find out their agenda? What clues would you have to listen out for?	

What incentives could you offer? What threats could you allude to facilitate movement?	
What signals could you look for from the other person?	
What vague signals could you use to respond positively or negatively to the signals you receive?	
What could you say or do to avoid being deflected from your goal?	
How will you know from the energy they bring to the negotiation how keen they are?	
When you need time to process the issues, how will you request a break?	

Remember that in the debate stage, everything is talked about in a vague manner to get a sense of their agendas and where their entry and exit points are.

Having completed your preparation grid and the checklist, you should be able to navigate your way through the debate stage. You will then be able to move on to make some proposals and use their reaction to your offers to gauge where a likely deal is to be made.

Step 3: Propose

Following the debate stage, take some time out to reflect on your discussions. Ask yourself the following questions

- What issues have you identified?
- Where do you think there is a deal to be done?
- What are your strong and weak points?
- What are their strong and weak points?

In the proposal stage, you will need to consider what you will trade in return for what you want. Here are some general guidelines to assist you at this stage.

- Keep things multifactorial and trade one thing for another.
- Focus on outcomes, not on the behaviour or personality of the other party.
- Respond to attempts to deflect you from your aim through flattery or criticism by using assertiveness techniques.
- Avoid criticising the other party or their offers – it delays achieving a successful outcome.
- Use the power of pausing to allow what you have said to 'settle in the air' and to be considered by the other party.
- Do not 'lay all your cards on the table'. If you do this you will have nowhere to go should your offer be rejected.
- Do not give up anything without getting something back in return.
- Do not make another offer before they have responded to your original offer.

What kind of things could you say to start off the offer process, bearing in mind that the structure of a proposal is always *if you do this for me, I will do this for you*.

What can you do to pace yourself during the proposal stage?

How will you keep track of the details of the proposals?

Once you are clear that there is an overlap on your offers and you have a real sense of where a deal may be struck you are ready to move on to making the bargain.

Step 4: Bargain

In the debate and proposal stage, your language should be very general, for example: 'I could possibly do this for you, if you do this for me' or 'What kind of offer did you have in mind?' When you are bargaining, the language is no longer vague. It is based on hard facts, figures, dates, targets, incentives and deadlines. Write down the bargain and ensure that you agree and have a shared perception about the outcome reached. The details you are hammering out here will form the basis of your contract.

At this stage, the main points to remember are:

- Nothing is settled until everything is settled.
- Be prepared to walk away from the negotiation if there is no overlap in your agendas, or if you cannot achieve a mutually beneficial agreement.

If the parties have understood the negotiation process and have an equal level of skill and self-confidence, the outcome should be win-win for both of them.

Taking action – negotiation

Using the prepared example above plan a negotiation and carry it out.

When will you be able to do this?

Who will you need to involve or consult?

What research do you need to do?

What have others achieved in a similar situation?

Who will start the process?

Move out of your comfort zone to do this.

DO IT!
Report back

What happened?

Were you happy with the outcome?

What would you do differently next time?

Reflection: What have you learnt about yourself and your ability to negotiate whilst working on this chapter?

Remember: As with all skills the only way to gain confidence and competence is to practice them until they feel natural to you.

As I mentioned in the People Skills Revolution, I very much see learning people skills as an equalisation process, giving the 'good guys' the same skills as those who use them in business and social situations all the time. Thinking about the director of finance in this example, if he had not been able to spot an opportunity and realise that his signature had a great value to the bank, he could have agreed to their first offer of £25k, which two other trusts had already accepted. He might even have been very satisfied with his ability to attract additional funds to a cash strapped organisation. Luckily in this instance this was not the case.

By lacking negotiation skills and the ability to spot an opportunity, professional negotiators 'get the better of' people both in the public and private sector, which can disadvantage their organisations to the tune of millions.

What this example demonstrates is that by reading the signals and using excellent negotiation skills, my client managed to achieve a result that many other people would only dream of.

What I noticed in this client and many others, is that once they know they can win, they often decide not to, particularly if the other party is not a skilled opponent, as the negotiators in this bank example. Instead they often chose to skill up the other side in disputes in order for them to engage with them on an equal (I positive, you positive) footing. This is when I started to realise that the next level up the continuum of interpersonal skills was conciliation.

Conciliation

Skilled negotiators love their ability to win and as the example in the last chapter shows, they love to find equal opponents with whom they can have a real negotiation tussle. Having said that, they are also able to identify people who are not able to identify the key issues and stand their ground to achieve their desired goal. This is when they start to become interested in conciliation. As one chief executive put it:

> '*I think the idea that there is a transition between negotiation and conciliation is true. You need to give in things (and I have done it deliberately) in order to be conciliatory. It is not good to win everything. You need to see the value of the longer-term relationship*'.

Once people have adopted a more conciliatory stance and have achieved negotiation skills it is a natural transition to be called on to assist others to work through conflict. Here their role is to see if they can find a point of agreement between two parties in conflict. Conciliation requires a high degree of skill. It also involves creating an environment of trust when trust is often in short supply. Because of the level of skill and self-control required to perform the conciliator role in a safe and effective manner, the function is often in the domain of lawyers and professional mediators.

If you are working from an 'I positive, you positive' perspective, and not trying to win at all costs, conciliation appears to be a quite natural progression from negotiation. When I first observed this happening with my clients, I noticed them going to have chats with their counterparts in other organisations and departments, who were technically on the opposing side to them. During these conversations they were assisting them to identify the key issues in the various agendas and then working with them to find the point at which both of them could agree and be satisfied with the outcome. Their counterparts, realising that they were now party to a helpful relationship rather than the antagonist one, started in turn to be more cooperative and work towards agreed shared agendas.

The major difference between assisting counterparts to be equal partners in negotiation in a conciliatory manner and conciliation, is that in conciliation there is likely to be a lot of emotions flying around and many of the reactions and descriptions may appear illogical.

Although conflict can take many forms, from major international disputes to family disagreements, the root causes behind the problem might be the same. These include:

- incompatible beliefs,
- no strategies for resolving conflict,
- cultural and religious differences,
- personality clashes,
- differences in communication style,
- a lack of respect for the circumstances of others.

Before I go on to the skills section of this chapter, I want to stress that conciliation is not for the faint hearted. It is also not about ego. It is about putting your skills and experience forward to assist two other people or parties to understand their different perspectives. Conciliators do this by adopting a safe approach, which systematically allows both parties to work through their issues in order to identify a point of agreement.

Readiness to perform the conciliator role

Before you start to become involved in conciliation you need to ask yourself a number of questions:

Can I maintain a completely 'I positive, you positive' position?

Do I have the ability to reserve judgement and not take sides?

Can I identify the real issues in the midst of possibly confusing dialogue, illogical explanations and heightened emotions?

Can I stick to a framework and work through it despite attempts to deflect me from my purpose?

Can I maintain clear boundaries between myself and the parties in dispute at all times?

Can I listen at the level of active and deep listening?

Can I dual process in the sense of actively listening whilst deciding where to take the conversation next?

Can I encourage others to describe events without emotional labeling or judgement?

Can I avoid getting drawn into the conflict by the parties wanting to get me on their side?

Can I establish my credibility as a conciliator?

Can I develop a relationship of trust?

Can I avoid the desire to offer advice?

Can I create an open, fair and equal environment?

Can I remain calm under pressure despite being provoked to react?

Can I see the person behind the problem?

Can I absorb, rather than respond, to criticism or attack?

Can I accept and respect the beliefs of others?

Can I ensure confidentiality?

Can I keep my language completely neutral?

Can I manage the expectations of both parties?

Can I ask pertinent questions that help people to reflect on, and understand, the issues behind their concerns?

Can I focus on facts and behaviour rather than emotions?

Can I avoid being deflected from the task to move parties towards agreement?

Can I summarise and write down agreements that have been reached?

Can I remain solution focused throughout the process?

You must be able to answer yes to all these questions to be ready to act in a conciliation role.

Conciliation – a step-by-step approach

In the People Skills Revolution, the conciliation process is based on the advice provided by ACAS[8](Advisory, Conciliation and Arbitration Service), which has been modified into a four-step approach to make it easy to follow.

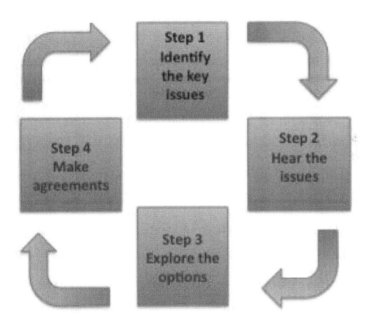

A Step by Step Approach to Conciliation

Step 1 Identify the key issues

Step 2 Hear the issues

Step 3 Explore the options

Step 4 Make agreements

---

8   Adapted from ACAS Mediation Model, ACAS 2007

- **Step 1:** Identify the key issues – in private, individual, confidential discussions with both parties, conciliator assists participants to recognise actions and behaviour behind the emotions that triggered the conflict
- **Step 2:** Hear the issues – create a safe environment for a joint meeting and use a clear framework to hear the issues so that each party has the opportunity to understand the perspective of the other
- **Step 3:** Explore the issues – having enabled each party to hear the other side to their story, the conciliator facilitates a discussion between the parties to identify a way forward
- **Step 4:** Make agreements – conciliator navigates parties towards solutions, summarises and writes down agreements

Conciliation – a practical example

The highly adapted example below describes a scenario, which is common in many working environments.

There has been a merger between two organisations. As a result a senior member of staff in one of the organisations has not achieved a corresponding role in the new company. Conflict has arisen between a middle manager and the senior manager within the new organisation. The middle manager has said that they will not work with the senior manager in the future unless a third person is present. A conciliator has been invited in assist in identifying a way forward.

Step 1: Identify the key issues

A two-hour meeting was arranged with each person to find out what was the cause of the disagreement.

Consideration was given to finding a comfortable room that was private and where interruptions could be avoided wherever possible.

During this meeting the conciliator established their credibility with the participants by explaining the process they had agreed to engage in. In doing this, they were careful to project an air of calm and confidence, which created a sense of trust in the process. The conciliator also checked that each individual was committed to working towards solutions to the problems they are facing. At the same time the conciliator explained that the meeting was confidential and that there would be no reporting back to anyone in the organisation unless they specifically agreed that this would happen.

The conciliator then asked each individual, in their separate meetings, to talk about the issues that had been concerning them. Given the fact that they were in conflict, it was no surprise that both parties were emotional. Here the conciliator's role is to encourage the parties to move from emotion and blame to behaviour and facts. The very process of talking to them in this way enabled them to focus on the key issues and took the emotional charge out of the situation.

During the individual discussions the conciliator took copious notes.

In the example above these were some of the issues that the participants highlighted.

Person one: comments about the conflict

- They are more senior than me they should not behave like this.
- Does not have a clear role.
- Is empire building.
- Has used aggressive language.
- They shouted at me in the middle of the office and refused to stop or leave when I asked them to.
- Decisions are made without being informed about them.
- Embarrassed in front of others by comments made by them.
- Seems to be an overlap in the own roles.
- Whatever ideas they come up with, we have already done it.
- They don't seem to be themselves.
- They contradict for the sake of it.
- They do have a lot of skill and expertise, which is not being tapped.
- Befriended them to start with and then felt they turned on me.
- Dogmatic language.
- They don't acknowledge the way I have been treated.

Person two: comments about the conflict

- Transition has been difficult.
- Feel that they discount what has been achieved in the past.
- Have been upset by the way I have been spoken to.
- Lack of clarity between roles.
- Incident blown up out of all proportion.

- I am used to operating in a much more senior role.
- Effectively I used to runing my own business, setting targets and achieving them.
- There have been some very critical emails.
- I have lots of things to offer but they are not interested.
- I have to go around people to get myself heard.
- There is a lot of pressure within the organisation.
- There is a lack of agreement about the way forward.
- Lack of support from above regarding my role.
- Lack of clarity between strategy and operations.
- Lack of engagement with issues I am leading on.

The discussions clearly served the purpose of clarifying the issues; they also had the effect of enabling both parties to express their emotions and consider what behaviour, behind the reactions, had triggered the conflict.

From these two discussions the following agenda was identified for the joint meeting where both parties were brought together to discuss the issues.

Agenda for meeting

1. Lack of clarity of roles
2. Organisational boundaries
3. Professional boundaries
4. Use of language and tone
5. Personal boundaries

Step 2: Hear the issues

Since both parties had identified a lack of clarity of roles as an issue, it was sensible to start there.

Person one had in effect initiated the conciliation by withdrawing from the situation, so it was sensible to start the meeting with them sharing their experience.

Organisational boundaries seemed more important to person two, therefore it was sensible for them to lead on sharing their experience.

It seemed sensible to keep all of the structural issues together, so professional boundaries was the third item on the agenda. This was a concern to both of them so for the sake of the balance and flow of the meeting, person one was invited to lead the sharing on this issue.

The use of language was very relevant to both of the parties. To maintain the pattern of alternating the agenda items, person 2 was invited to lead on this.

Finally since personal boundaries was of particular relevance to person one they were invited to lead on this item.

In describing their perspective of the issues, both parties were encouraged to share separately without making any comment or interrupting the other party.

Step 3: Explore the issues

One way to explore the options is to do this after each of the agenda items. The alternative would be to work through all of the agenda items alternatively sharing their perspectives and then to move onto exploring the options.

Which ever approach you select, the core process, which I have mentioned many times throughout this book is: Where are you now? Where do you want to be? And finally, how are you going to get there?

Personally I prefer to get all the issues out on the table to get a sense of the overall situation and then work through the agenda items again to help the participants decide where they would like to be, then help people focus down on how to get there.

In this scenario, the participants agreed that they were not in a position between them to resolve the clarity of role issues although they did acknowledge that it was the root cause of a lot of problems between them. They agreed to write down their perceived roles and acknowledge where the overlap caused problems.

In terms of organisational boundaries, person one accepted that person two required greater clarity about this. The two organisations, as they merged into one, had very different ways of operating – one was more hierarchical than the other and clarifying the differences and why they reacted differently was useful. Some of the problems they were experiencing were clearly about semantics. Person one also acknowledged that person two had a great deal of skills and expertise that were not being used in the current organisational structure.

When talking about professional boundaries, it was obvious that some of the problems arose because person two had to go through person one to get their job done. It was agreed that person two needed to put some significant effort into building the relationship with person one's manager.

Use of language and tone. This was a significant issue for them both. During the course of the discussion, it was clear that both of them had not treated the other with the degree of respect that they should have been able to expect from their colleagues. They agreed to pay particular attention to focusing on facts and taking the emotion out of their interactions.

Finally on the question of personal boundaries. Person one felt that person two had acted inappropriately when they shouted at them in the middle of the office and refused to stop or leave when requested to do so. Person two acknowledged that although they saw the incident very differently, they would apologise to person one if they had perceived the situation in this manner.

Step 4: Make agreements

The agreements fell out of the discussion that had previously taken place. The role of the conciliator is to bring the agreements together so that they can be written down and that the participants can commit to them.

The agreements in this scenario were:

- Write down their perceived roles.
- Identify the overlap in roles and recognise the problems caused by this.
- Acknowledge each other's skills.
- Continue to clarify differences between the two organisations in terms of policies and structures. Recognise that this process could be useful in establishing a new culture for the merged organisation.
- Person two agreed to take action to improve the relationship with person one's manager.
- They both agreed to pay particular attention to focusing on facts and to take the emotion, judgement and labeling out of their verbal and written communications.
- They agreed to meet regularly and with a clear agenda to discuss issues of joint concern.

Assessing your readiness to become a conciliator

To become an effective conciliator you need to have a wide range of people skills, combined with the readiness to make other peoples' agenda your agenda.

Are you sure you have developed the skills of assertiveness, influence and negotiation sufficiently to appear a 'natural' in those areas to other people?

What would motivate you to become a conciliator?

Having read the chapter on conciliation what skills or qualities do you still need to develop?

One of the most important of these skills is to be able to listen to a stream of information, which may at times appear to be very random and rambling, then to be able to boil it down to a number of key issues that have relevance and can be agreed upon by both parties.

What can you do to prepare for this particular challenge?

What other experiences would prepare you for the role?

What skills could you practice prior to being asked to conciliate?

Who could you talk to who has performed this role already?

What could you say to the parties when you meet them individually to explain the process you will be engaging in, develop trust and gain their commitment.

Conciliation – planning a conciliation conversation

Step 1: Identify the key issues

The aim of this step is to talk to each of the parties individually in order to agree the agenda for the joint meeting. At the joint meeting you will use this agenda to enable each party to share their perception of the issue under discussion.

It is important that people understand the process that they are entering into and that it is managed fairly to ensure equality. It is also important that there is a sensible reason for each process decision that you make.

What would you say to each individual when you meet them separately, to explain the process to them and establish a relationship of trust?

What would you say to encourage each individual to talk about the problems that have occurred between them?

How would you listen closely to what is said and take notes whilst at the same time working out where to take the conversation next?

How would you ensure that you have given them sufficient time and space to explore all of the issues?

As you speak to each person individually you will want to find out if they have ideas or suggestions to improve the situation. How would you ask this question?

What would you say to the other person to give yourself some time and space to reflect on the key issues and create agenda items for the joint meeting?

Based on the information given by both parties separately, when you bring them together would you plan to hear all of the issues on your agenda, one by one, as a complete step and then move onto steps three (explore the options) and four (make agreements)?

or

Would you hear each of the issues separately and then move on to exploring the options and making agreements for each issue on the agenda?

This decision will be based on the number of items on the agenda, the complexity of the issues, your own skill to maintain your focus whilst dealing with a number of factors simultaneously, and your ability to identify the best time to move them towards making agreements.

Step 2: Hear the issues

How would you decide the order of the agenda items and who would talk first in the discussions?

How would you present the agenda for the meeting and agree the process that the meeting will follow?

What actions could you take to keep the discussions on track?

What actions could you take to ensure that equality is maintained between the parties at all times?

How would you ensure that your own personal biases and preferences do not get in the way of your ability to act as an impartial facilitator?

How would you resist the temptation to jump in with your own interpretations and suggestions?

How would you ensure that you stick to the process you have agreed with both parties?

Step 3: Explore the issues

Once both parties have had the opportunity to hear both sides of the issues, what would you say to them to signal that you will move on to exploring the options?

How would you encourage them to suggest possible ways to resolve their differences, whilst avoiding offering any solutions yourself?

What could you do or say to prompt further suggestions?

If they are reluctant to participate in exploring options to resolve the situation, you might want to remind them that at the outset they did agree to engage in the conciliation process.

Once you have some viable suggestions on the table you are ready to move on to making agreements.

Step 4: Make agreements

The agreements that the parties make between them are owned by the participants, not by you as the conciliator. For this reason they need to be clear and concise, documenting who is doing what and by when.

Before you write down the agreements, how will you check that what you think they have agreed is in alignment with what they believe has been agreed?

How, and in what form, will you leave the agreements with the parties?

Taking action – conciliation

Unless you have been trained to be a conciliator and have been designated to perform this role, it is unlikely that you will be formally approached to mediate between two parties unless you have gained a reputation for taking on this role.

Initially you will gain experience in this role by listening to people telling their stories and trying to work out what you think are the key issues behind their emotional responses. It would be helpful if you could move them from a position of blame to describing the behaviour and how it affected them.

As we have seen, listening in itself is a therapeutic process, so what could you do to practise this skill without taking on the formal conciliator role?

In what situations might you be able to practice the listening, questioning and facilitation skills required to become an effective conciliator?

When will you be able to do this?

DO IT!
Report back

What happened?

Were you satisfied with the outcome?

What feedback did you receive from other people about the usefulness of your approach?

What would you do differently next time?

Reflection: Acting as a conciliator requires a huge amount of personal self-awareness. You will need to combine a very high level of interpersonal skills with the ability to gradually move the parties in conflict from emotional reactions to logical joint problem solving. This involves creating an environment of trust, assisting them to identify the issues, guiding the process using a framework, looking for signals and funneling the discussion towards an agreement that both parties can sign up to.

What did you learn about yourself and your ability to become a conciliator whilst working through this chapter?

Remember: Acting as a conciliator is something that will challenge your beliefs about yourself and other people. It also provides you with the opportunity to observe human behaviour at very close quarters. In doing this it is likely that you will notice patterns in people's behaviour that you will not have noticed before. You will notice when people say and do things, which create drama and use language which triggers a reaction in the other person.

When conciliating, it is not your role to act on any of the patterns that you may have identified, but these patterns and your reactions to these patterns, will, I believe, contribute to your growing sense of who you are and what you are about.

It will also make you aware of your own judgements and assumptions about people and stimulate your thoughts about who you are and what you stand for.

Taking a stand

In the People Skills Revolution I mention that I have been fortunate to coach some clients with excellent interpersonal skills and to have been able to work with them over a long period of time – often many years. The people who cease to be clients often become friends, so I am also able to keep in touch with them and see how they are progressing in their careers and in their own personal development. In fact, now they often teach me more things than I teach them.

When I first observed the continuum of interpersonal skills, I based it on my own experience and the experience of my clients as I saw them develop. I then used it to pre-empt the learning in others rather than simply track it. This turned out to be a highly effective, step-by-step approach to developing the more sophisticated people skills. The idea of an incremental build in skills led me to suggest that assertiveness underpins all interpersonal skills and that once these are developed, people would naturally go on to develop the skills of influencing, negotiation and conciliation. It was my curiosity that led me to wonder if there were any other levels past this point on the continuum.

The next stage up the continuum of interpersonal skills I identified was making peace. This was based on reading about Michael Young[9] who, when public affairs director of Consolidated Gold Fields, was challenged by Oliver Tambo, co-founder of the African National Congress, to set up all party talks. Taking considerable personal risk, he facilitated a process that led to the peaceful transition to black majority rule in South Africa in 1994. Young's approach was mirrored in the work of Jonathan Powell and George J Mitchell, who were instrumental in establishing a series of talks that achieved peace in Northern Ireland in 2007.

What seemed to set the peacemakers apart was their reluctant readiness to take on challenges that might involve huge personal risk that other people would walk away from. So I became interested in the process, which encouraged them to combine their highly sophisticated people skills with being prepared to navigate warring parties through a process towards peace. This decision point is illustrated by Michael Young when he talked about the political situation in South Africa, before independence.

---

9   Extract from an interview with Michael Young broadcast on the Channel 4 website, 25 April 2009

> *'It is not enough to believe that something is evil – you have to actually rationalise and say what can I do with my skill set in the area in which I operate to do something practical to change it'.*

These sentiments are also echoed in the words of George J Mitchell[10], US Senator, when talking about his decision to become involved in the Northern Ireland peace process.

> *'I was in a position to help. I didn't seek or expect it, but it was a reality. How could I turn away from it now? I had been taught that each human being has an obligation to help those in need; I had preached the same thing to young Americans countless times. Did I really believe what I said? And if I did leave, and the war resumed, how could I reconcile myself to the deaths that would result, deaths that might have been prevented if I had stuck with it?'*

When I wrote the original book, I admit that the section on making peace was largely a prediction of where the next logical step might be, and I did believe that if my clients continued on the route they were going that this would lead them on to develop the skills of the peacemaker.

Having identified the actions of the peacemakers, I also believed that there was a stage before making peace that turned skilled conciliators into peacemakers. This is the point where they work out who they are and what they believe in, and decide to take action to improve the community around them.

In other words, there appeared to be a stage between conciliation and making peace, which transfigured people with highly developed people skills into potential peacemakers. The difference appeared to be a very clear sense of who they were and what they stood for. I called this stage Taking a Stand on the continuum of interpersonal skills.

Up to this point, people's values and beliefs are whirring away in the background, influencing their behaviour in an unconscious manner. At the stage of taking a stand, people start to become very conscious of their beliefs and values

10 Making Peace, William Heinemann 1999

and use them to guide their actions when navigating through difficult situations. They also gain an ability to act whilst resisting considerable pressure from parties who have different agendas to their own.

When I wrote the People Skills Revolution, few of my clients had reached this point and nor had I. In the intervening two years it has been extremely interesting to see how my clients have progressed, and I can now report that more of them are entering the stage of asking themselves: 'Who am I and what do I believe in?' This led them to act in a way that was driven by their principles and values. As a result they left organisations if their mode of operations did not align with their beliefs and values, stepped into highly challenging roles because they felt they could make a difference, and withstood considerable pressure from board colleagues to say 'no' when they did not agree with their stance. They are also increasingly following their dreams and achieving success in their careers that previously they would not have anticipated. Often they were being thrust into these roles by circumstances, rather than applying for the positions in the usual way.

A number of them are also making peace. Not on the national and political scale mentioned in the book, but using a peacemaking process to bring conflicting groups together to work towards a common goal. In doing this, they are breaking down the barriers that have existed for decades, and established an agenda that all parties can buy into.

I wanted to take a closer look at what was involved in the taking a stand stage, and have decided that this is a far more complex transition than it appears. At this point three things seem to happen.

1. A desire to conduct a personal inventory of their values, principles, skills and readiness to act.
2. A fascination for people, almost in an observer role. As they manage to detach from the game-playing that embroils them in drama, they become interested in what influences others to act the way they do. In doing this they are able to take the behaviour of others less personally and to see each interaction from an 'I positive, you positive' perspective.
3. They begin to notice how others can move them off centre, and become interested in how to remain calm and in control when facing extreme provocation.

To assist with this stage I have included exercises that will help you to reflect on who you are and what you stand for. I have also included a section on dealing with challenging behaviour. In the People Skills Revolution, I deliberately glossed over impoverished interpersonal skills in order to focus on the beliefs and skills necessary to achieve exceptional results.

More recently, I have come to understand that, at the level of taking a stand for what you believe in and peacemaking, people have an in-depth understanding of human behaviour and how it impacts on others. They also manage to maintain an 'I positive, you positive' stance, which, as I mentioned in the beginning of the book, is a fundamental prerequisite to becoming more assertive and accumulating all the other more sophisticated skills.

I now believe that understanding apparently illogical behaviour is a basic building block to making peace. In the People Skills Revolution, I included a section on 'defusing the arch-manipulator', which is an approach that I worked out with my clients to assist them when they came across some very difficult and slippery characters. Being able to deal with them successfully gave them a huge degree of confidence and made them realise that, if they could handle the arch-manipulator's behaviour, they could handle the behaviour of virtually anyone.

Having worked in the field of personal development for many years, I believe that the number of people who are arch-manipulators, in the sense that I talk about in the book, is incredibly small. What is clear though from the comments I have received from readers of the original book, is that game playing and bullying is extremely widespread, and they have found the advice presented on how to deal with the arch-manipulator very useful.

I have, therefore, decided to integrate the information on dealing with the arch-manipulator into this chapter, but also to add a section on game playing and introduce a concept called the drama triangle. This helps to explain some dysfunctional behaviour you will observe and perhaps become embroiled in. It also gives you different choices on how to deal with it. I am sure it will resonate with many people.

This includes a step-by-step approach to moving away from the drama brought about by games and allows you to focus on building healthy 'I positive, you positive' relationships. You will notice that in rewriting the script of a game, basic assertiveness is still the underlying skill in changing your behaviour and in influencing the behaviour of others.

Finally clients who are moving on to this stage are increasingly asking me how to stay centred and calm in the face of, often, huge provocation from other people. I have started to use meditation to enable me to stand back and observe myself and situations rather than become embroiled in chaos or dramas. I recommend the same technique, which I have found very useful, to my clients, so far with promising results. You will find this technique at the end of this chapter.

If you follow this section through from beginning to end, I guarantee that you will deepen your awareness of yourself and others.

Who are you? – an inventory

1. Who are you?

2. What do you believe in?

3. What skills do you possess that other people may not have developed yet?

4. What have been the critical turning points in your life when you made decisions about your future and the way you would like to live your life?

   Event   Why critical?

5. What are your principles/values – the factors that help you decide what is important to you, how you govern your life and to make decisions?

6. When was the last time you took a stand over something, or resisted considerable pressure to do something you believed was not right?

7. What happened and what principles or ideals were at stake for you?

8. What, personally, do you think is wrong with society as a whole (or your particular part of it)?

9. What dramas or disruptions take place around you on a regular basis?

10. Who would you identify as the main characters in this drama and why?

   First list the characters and then explain why you believe they are difficult or on your side.

                                            Why?

   Difficult characters

   On your side

11. What can you do about these dramas?

12. What are your hopes and dreams for society, your department, family or yourself?

13. What can you do to make these hopes and dreams come true?

14. If this society, department, family or group was a blank page with no history, what would you create on it?

15. What quick wins could you achieve?

16. Any finally, what can you do with the skills set you have, to make a difference?

Dealing with impoverished interpersonal skills

Underpinning the art of making peace is the skill of bringing warring parties together to focus on a common agenda. Conciliators then establish a safe process can buy into, which keeps the talks on track even when the going gets tough. In the time it takes to talk, all parties also learn to value themselves and value other people. To facilitate this effectively, a peacemaker must not side with one party over the others or get caught up in dramas and hostility.

The skills of conciliation help to keep the parties and the conciliator safe. Becoming a peacemaker requires a much higher degree of control over a sustained period of time to navigate through the games and manipulation that are likely to be present, whilst at the same time understanding human nature sufficiently to maintain an 'I positive, you positive' position.

I hope that the information on game playing and the arch-manipulator, which follows, will not only enable you to detach from your own dramas but also to assist other people in conflict to do this too.

Understanding the drama triangle

Based on the concept of Transactional Analysis devised by Eric Berne in the 1960s and outlined in his book 'Games People Play'[11], this therapeutic approach looks at human interaction in terms of parent, adult, child states. In his book, Berne suggests that we play games to get our needs for attention met, when we are unable to get them met in an authentic and straightforward manner.

'Games People Play' identified over 30 games, but some of the most popular and descriptive ones are:

Alcoholic	I was only trying to help you
Addict	Look how hard I've tried
Ain't it Awful	Now I've got you son of a bitch
Blemish	See what you made me do
Debtor	Why don't you – yes, but
Kick me	Wooden leg
If it weren't for you	

All of us play games at some level. Each of the games involves the players taking up a starting position of persecutor, rescuer or victim. Berne suggested that everyone who plays a game will switch to every other position in the game so

11 Penguin 2010

that the person playing victim in one round will eventually play rescuer, or then persecutor, in later rounds.

Games are played outside of our awareness. It is almost as though we are wearing an invisible 'T' shirt with persecutor, rescuer or victim on it. This slogan can be subconsciously read by others and lets them know our preferred start position, and enables us to find the player who will take on the corresponding role in our game without us realising that we are doing this.

The definition of a persecutor is someone who seems like a critical or controlling parent – an aggressor who acts out the unconscious slogan 'I can make you feel bad'.

The definition of a rescuer is someone who seems like a nurturing parent – an apparently nice and helpful person who acts out the unconscious slogan 'I can make you feel good'.

A person is rescuing when he or she is:

1. Doing something they don't want to do.
2. Doing something they have not been asked to do.
3. Is doing more than 50 per cent of the work.
4. Is not asking for what he/she wants.

The definition of a victim is someone who seems like a helpless or adapted child – an apparently hopeless and powerless person who gives his or her power to others, who acts out the unconscious slogan 'you can make me feel good or bad'.

Both persecutor and rescuer positions are played from the 'one up', or 'I am positive, you are negative' position.

The victim position is played from the 'one down' or 'I am negative, you are positive' position.

The basic structure of a game is:
- Identification of a victim (either for the persecutor or the rescuer).
- A hook (a way of hooking the unsuspecting mark).
- A switch (when one of the game players – victim, persecutor or rescuer changes the direction of the transaction).
- Confusion – when the players can't understand how they got to this position and have an 'old familiar feeling that they have been there before'.
- Return to original position – all parties feel uncomfortable in the switch position and move back to original positions where the game starts again.

All of us play games, and all of us play from a preferred starting position. Games can be fairly innocuous, or for people with a tendency to play more dangerous games, can escalate into murder or warfare.

In 1968, Stephen Karpman further developed the concept of game theory in an article called 'Fairy Tales and Script Drama Analysis'[12] by introducing the idea of the Drama Triangle. In this article, Karpman published a simple and illuminating diagram to illustrate how games unfold. From time to time, I send this model to clients to help them understand and disengage from the dynamics of difficult and repeating situations they may find themselves in. I particularly like this model because you do not have to understand a great deal about transactional analysis to understand the behaviour it is describing. It seems to have an innate wisdom about it that most people seem to grasp straightaway.

The diagram below shows Karpman's Drama Triangle and illustrates the shifts in position, which occur when the games are being played.

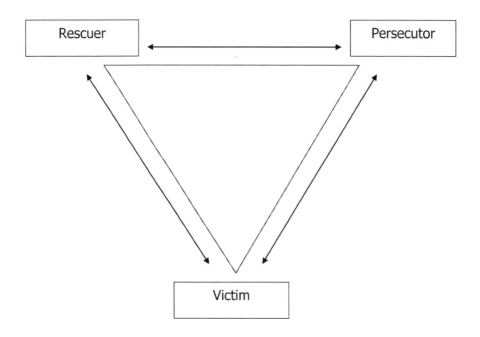

Transactional Analysis itself is a complete study of human behaviour, which can be very useful to help interpret our own actions and the actions of others. However, I have found that when I explain the drama triangle to my clients they intuitively seem to understand the underlying principle behind the approach and can use it to make different choices about their behaviour.

12 Transactional Analysis Bulletin, 7(26)

The drama triangle – a practical example

Here is an example, which starts from the persecutor position. A person who is persecuting picks an adult or child who has a tendency to act like a victim and niggles them and niggles them in very low key and subtle ways (the hook) until the victim has had enough and very obviously turns into a persecutor (switch). The persecutor then acts like a victim (switch) and invites sympathy from third parties and looks gloatingly at the previous victim implying: 'Now I've got you, you son of a bitch.' Very soon both parties will move back into their preferred role and if nothing changes the game will start again.

I once worked in a department where the secretary controlled the department. You could not get a paper clip without having her permission. She also took it in turns to persecute people in the department, and to my shame, I did not defend colleagues when they were in her trajectory. Nor did they defend me when it was my time to play victim in the game. What she did was to make small criticisms, which none of us challenged, until one day the cumulative effect of insults and put downs became too much. When it was our turn to be in the game we exploded, moving from victim to persecutor. When the boss asked us what was the problem, all of the reasons for our eruptions sounded so trivial that we looked stupid. This left the secretary able to look at us as if to say 'see what I have to put up with; they just get angry over nothing' – moving from persecutor to victim.

A few days later the game would usually start again but this time involving someone else. It was as if we were continually acting out the game: 'Now I have got you, you son of a bitch.'

The effect of this situation was that the department was in constant drama with mature adults walking on egg shells and reduced to the status of quivering wrecks. At this point I came across the concept of the drama triangle. When I moved into an observer position, I could see the game unfold. I began to spot the 'hooks' and know when my personal buttons where being pressed. Although it took a considerable amount of self-control, I learnt not to react when provoked. On one occasion, I even remember sitting on my hands and counting to ten to avoid getting caught up in the game. What was fascinating for me, after this event, was that the other members of the department also learnt to disengage from the dynamic, with the result that the secretary became a much more equal and involved member of the team.

I hope that this simple example from my own experience will assist you to understand the drama triangle as it is played out.

Here is another example.

I can do CVs for people, and used to enjoy offering to do them for people without them asking (rescuing). I used to sell the idea to them (the hook) and then put a lot of work into them. When I completed and sent them to people, sometimes I did not hear from them, not even a thank you. I would then often find out that they had used them to significantly improve their salary or get a better job.

I began to feel very resentful (the switch) to those people and criticised their lack of consideration (victim). If I had raised it with them, it is possible that they would have tried to rescue me by apologising and trying to make me feel better. In this instance, I would be playing 'look how hard I've tried' or if they had persecuted me, I would be playing 'I was only trying to help you'.

Alternatively I could have moved positions to persecutor and play the 'after all I have done for you' card.

Rather than move back into the rescuer position, in fact I learnt not to rescue in future with regard to CVs and stepped off the triangle.

Games create chaos, conflict, excitement and of course drama. They also serve to reinforce negative life positions, or scripts, and you see how they fit in with the negative thought processes that we covered in the chapter on Changing Negative Beliefs.

A simple way to explore the games you may play

Are you aware of playing games yourself?

If you are, what is your preferred starting position – rescuer, victim, persecutor?

Who do you tend to play this game with?

Do any of the game titles fit the game you tend to play?

What is it that happens over and over again in your interactions with others?

How does it start?

Then what happens?

What happens next?

How does it end?

How do you feel when it ends?

How do you think the other person feels when it ends?

Playing games – A step-by-step approach to stepping out of the drama

Getting out of a game can be difficult since the more you fight to get out of it the more you may dig yourself deeper. This guide should help you to give up this destructive and non-productive pattern.

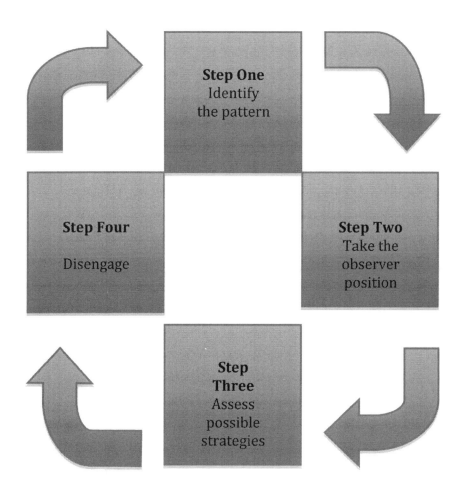

Step One
Identify
the pattern

Step Four

Disengage

Step Two
Take the
observer
position

Step Three
Assess
possible
strategies

- **Step 1:** Identify the patterns
- **Step 2:** Take the observer position
- **Step 3:** Assess possible strategies to deal with the situation
- **Step 4:** Take action to disengage

Step 1: Identify the patterns

First of all we need to be aware that we are in a dysfunctional triangle and recognise our tendency to be there. We must also feel dissatisfied enough about the situation for it to be worthwhile to provoke a change and risk temporary discomfort in ourselves and the other players.

Step 2: Take the observer position

We need to put some distance between ourselves and the situation in order to clearly identify the role each player is playing – this is called the observer or meta-position.

At the observer step, what you are looking for is the 'hook'. This is the action that you or the other person takes that signals the beginning of a game. I see this very much like the 'clunk' noise you hear when you are on a roller coaster and you are belted into your seat. The ride is about to start and you know that there is no going back.

If the game continues anyway – you have taken rather than avoided the hook – observe the behaviour that follows.

Step 3: Assess possible strategies

Mentally analyse the situation by using a number of possible strategies, i.e. humour, search for positive intentions behind behaviours, realising that both are caught in the game, believing that you are no better or worse than anybody else. Acknowledging that this is unconscious behaviour, which has been learnt and can therefore be unlearnt.

Step 4: Take action to disengage

Disengage – notice the hook and do nothing. Step out of the drama. Respond from your adult – make different decisions/choices. Allow people to sort out their own problems. Stop trying to blame others and take responsibility for yourself and no one else.

Finally if appropriate, share your observations with the other players to help them disengage from the game.

Using the step-by-step approach to stepping out of the drama triangle, analyse and plan your route out of the game.

Planning to step out of a drama triangle

Step 1: Identify the patterns

What recurring (and usually destructive) pattern is played out with you and the other person, which leaves you with an 'old familiar feeling that you have been here before'?

What are the consequences of this behaviour for you and the other person?

Stepping out of games takes time, energy, patience, persistence and commitment. Are you prepared to make this investment in changing your behaviour?

Step 2: Take the observer position

What actions can you take to move from being a player in the game to an observer of the drama?

What can you do to resist the clear 'hooks' you will experience from the other player to ensure that you remain part of the game?

What can you do to physically distance yourself from the situation?

What can you say (or not say) to psychologically distance yourself from the situation?

Step 3: Assess possible strategies

Your possible options for seeing the game differently include:

- approaching it with humour,
- searching for positive intentions behind the behaviours,
- realising that both are caught in the game and are party to the outcomes,
- believing that you are no better or worse than anybody else,
- acknowledging that this is unconscious behaviour, which has been learnt and can be unlearnt.

Which of these options is the most appropriate to your own situation?

Step 4: Take action to disengage

When you step out of the game, you will receive some very powerful invitations to encourage you to keep playing. Your counter part will probably 'up the ante' to keep the *status quo* as it is and the usual subconscious hooks will become stronger and more apparent – particularly if you have successfully moved towards the observer position.

It may take a great deal of self-restraint to resist re-entering the game, but knowing you are in one helps you to do this. The moment you re-engage with the players is the moment that you step back into the drama.

What will you need to do when faced with this extreme provocation?

What different actions can you take, and what different choices can you make to stop blaming others, allow adults to sort out their own problems, and take responsibility for yourself and no one else?

Do you believe you have the time, energy, patience, persistence and commitment to change your behaviour?

Are you prepared to make this investment?

Remember: I hope that having a greater understanding of the drama triangle and game playing will give you some more options in how you approach others. By adjusting your behaviour to avoid becoming embroiled in repeating negative patterns, you will substantially improve your ability to act in an 'I positive, you positive' manner and stop operating from a rescuer, persecutor and victim position. The step-by-step approach will help you to disengage from most games you will come across and enable you to become calmer and more in control in a wider variety of situations.

The arch-manipulator

When working with clients who understood the nature of games and had excellent interpersonal skills, a few of them came across people whose behaviour they just could not deal with. These people who we labeled 'arch-manipulators' could create chaos where none had existed before, set one party against another when before they got on just fine, and generally threw the organisation and its employees into disarray. It was difficult to see why they did this and we probably never did fathom the reason for their actions. It could be to appear more intelligent than they were, it could be to hide a perceived weakness, it could be motivated by a need to control. It could also be to hide some wrong doing by diverting attention away from the scene of the action by creating a smokescreen.

What ever the reason, the impact of these characters on the organisations they popped up in was the same. They took energy and resources away from doing the job in hand and meeting the business objectives. Instead, people became obsessed with defending their actions, recovering from unjustified attacks, creating an audit trail and talking about their experiences with colleagues.

It is clear from the feedback I have received from the People Skills Revolution that readers found this chapter particularly helpful. It was also apparent that they often went straight to this chapter, since they had suffered from bullying behaviour in the past. Many people wrote to me to tell me that they wished that they had had access to this information earlier on in their working and personal lives.

Despite this feedback, I still maintain that the number of people who are arch-manipulators in the true sense of the word is tiny. I hope that the section on the drama triangle will contribute another perspective and assist people to make different choices. I think the people we identified as arch-manipulators combined the tactics of the game 'now I have got you, you son of a bitch' with highly developed skills of manipulation, which they use to their own ends in an extremely destructive manner. So they can be charming one minute and highly volatile the next. They can also present very different faces to different people, which reinforces the sense of confusion.

Whilst games are played outside of peoples' awareness, I have a feeling that arch-manipulators are quite conscious of their behaviour and have learnt the skills of manipulation in the same way as I am encouraging you to learn the skills of influence. They use a unique blend of aggression and manipulation to treat people like pawns in their own personal chess game.

How to recognise an arch-manipulator

Imagine you are a highly skilled individual who considers that you can always get your point across in an intelligent, considered and structured manner, which most people can understand and accept, even if they do not always agree with you. Then you come across one of these characters who seem to have a way of deflecting and reframing everything you say to the detriment of your argument. I believe it is only natural to think that these people are highly intelligent, because mostly you do not feel flummoxed in this way. You will then feel that you are missing something and must just concentrate more.

In other words, they gradually and subtly start taking over your working life and your thoughts. It is precisely this level of surprise, shock and disbelief that lets arch-manipulators get away with their strategies.

From listening to my clients who were experiencing problems with these difficult people – or arch-manipulators – they appeared to share some common factors.

1. They were often highly charismatic characters who appeared out of nowhere with no formal recruitment process in place.
2. They sometimes claimed overseas qualifications and experience, but due to the lack of formal recruitment process and the sense of authority they commanded, these claims were often not checked.
3. They had people running around in circles and erupting in emotional outbursts, while this person sat back and watched it happen.
4. They often made their interventions in the name of greater efficiency, proposed new structures because the current ones were not working, and suggested that people were not doing their job properly.
5. They rarely had a significant project or chunk of work to do, when all the tasks were allocated.
6. They cloaked all of their contributions in terms of the authority gained from their patron or other person in authority.

7. They make incredibly general contributions whilst making very specific criticisms.

8. They had an ability to identify each person's 'Achilles heel' or weak spot.

9. They would get the most even-tempered of people swinging into action to defend themselves.

10. They knew what buttons to press to create chaos, and they appeared to take a great deal of pleasure in walking into a room, pulling the pin on the hand grenade, then stepping back to see the result of their actions.

11. They gained pleasure from identifying how they could wheedle themselves into an organisation or group and gain huge satisfaction from manipulating it, just because they could.

12. They also appeared to have a 'hold' on the leader of the organisation or group, although they seemed unlikely to go for the leadership role itself.

13. They used the reflected, unappointed or unelected power that was conferred on them by the leader to destabilise the organisation.

After months of discussing the phenomenon, and helping my clients to cope with the chaos that these people generated, we were able to piece together an effective strategy for dealing with the arch-manipulators.

Defusing the arch-manipulator

The key to understanding this behaviour came when one of my clients became interested in the strategies of powerful men. He told me about a publication called 'The Art of Controversy – Volume 5' by Arthur Schopenhauer[13], who (writing in 1831) described a form of interaction called 'the Controversial Dialectic'. This is defined as the art of disputing, and of disputing in such a way as to hold one's own, irrespective of whether or not you are right. In this extended essay, Schopenhauer identified 38 common tricks and dodges used by people who he perceived lacked the learning, intelligence and self-respect to present their case in a logical, reasoned, truthful, just and yielding manner.

The 38 stratagems that Schopenhauer set out for winning arguments can be paraphrased as follows.

1. Exaggerate then discredit the opponent's position.
2. Pick out a word or phrase that stands out, then misinterpret it.
3. Attack something different from what is asserted.
4. Conceal the game by gradually gaining admissions and then mingle premises and admissions into the conversation.

13 The Penn State Electronic Classics Series 2005

5. Draw a true conclusion from a false premise.

6. Discredit truth by making sweeping generalised statements about the subject area in general.

7. Ask a number of wide-ranging questions at once, so that people will not notice gaps or mistakes in the argument.

8. Make the opponent angry, so that he is incapable of good judgement and of perceiving where his advantage lies.

9. Put questions in a different order than the conclusion to be drawn from them requires.

10. If someone continually says 'no', ask the question in the opposite to get them to say 'yes'.

11. Use support for particular cases to suggest support of generalised cases.

12. Use phrases, words or metaphors that suggest a positive interpretation of the preferred position.

13. Give an exaggerated and less favourable view of a counter-proposition.

14. When the argument is not going their way, claim victory anyway.

15. Suggest seemingly absurd propositions from the opponent's arguments.

16. Say the equivalent of: 'If you are not happy about the situation, why don't you do something about it (e.g. leave, resign, speak up)?'

17. If the opponent presses counter-proof, advance a subtle distinction.

18. Interrupt, break or divert a successful line of enquiry.

19. If pressed to find an objection in a winning argument, make a generalised criticism of the human condition.

20. Draw final conclusions themself, even though some of the premises are lacking.

21. Counter superficial and misleading arguments with equally unsound arguments.

22. Create a circular argument, where the conclusion appears both at the beginning and the end of the argument.

23. Irritate their opponent into exaggerating their argument through contradiction and contention.

24. State a false deductive argument.

25. Identify a single instance to the contrary to overturn their argument.

26. Turn their opponent's arguments against them.

27. If an argument accidentally causes anger, press the point more to exploit the weak spot.

28. Use ridicule and laughter against an opponent to get the audience on your side.

29. If the argument is being lost, create a diversion.

30. Appeal to authority or universally held opinion, rather than to reason.
31. Declare a lack of understanding of the opponent's argument.
32. Link their opponent's argument with an 'odious' category or 'ism'.
33. State 'that is all very well in theory, but it will not work in practice'.
34. If a weakness is identified and reduces them to silence, press the point more.
35. Demonstrate that the opponent's viewpoint is contradictory to their self-interest.
36. Puzzle and bewilder, by blasting with words assumed to have meaning.
37. Refute a faulty proof to a correct argument, and use it to discredit the whole position.
38. Become personally insulting and rude.

As you can see, the whole premise of the Controversial Dialectic is 'I positive, you negative', so it is essentially an aggressive stance. I have included these stratagems not to suggest you learn them, but to make you aware of their existence. Once you realise you are dealing with someone who likes to indulge in this type of interaction, you can prepare some more considered responses.

At a very primitive level, as human beings we are programmed to defend ourselves or attack the opponent if threatened. Faced with the very sophisticated and skilled stimulus used by a very tiny proportion of the population, people with highly developed interpersonal skills find themselves either defending themselves or attacking the other person.

This may involve doing masses of additional work that they know is unnecessary, or justifying their actions for reasons that they cannot quite explain. Alternatively, they become very emotional or angry, despite all their efforts to control their reactions.

What arch-manipulators do is create chaos where none existed before, and know what 'buttons' to press to get people to act emotionally and fall out with people that they used to previously get on with. When this over reaction occurs, the spotlight is taken off the manipulator who can then carve out a pathway to their goal.

Defusing the arch-manipulator – a practical example

In the chapter on assertiveness, we left a finance director successfully saying 'no' to an aggressive department head wanting additional funding without producing a business plan. If the department head was an arch-manipulator, that would not be the end of the story.

The department head would continue to work behind the scenes to undermine the finance director. They would arrange, or just turn up at meetings where the director is finance is present, where the agenda has no relevance to them, and ask the director impossible questions and then verbally attack their response, which will weaken them and put them on their guard for the next time they meet.

They will have organised a meeting as soon after this personally challenging event as possible, and raise their issue again whilst their victim is still licking their wounds.

They will drop in and visit people who interact with and work close to the director. After a pleasant chat they will gently suggest that they question the competence of the finance director and plant insecurities in their mind about the director of finance's role, which these people will feel compelled to express at meetings. When writing up documents or emails they will deliberately misinterpret something the director has done or said and include an implied criticism, which the recipient would feel compelled to respond to. They ask deceptively simple questions of the director and his incredibly busy team, which appear to be relevant but will involve a considerable amount of extra work with very little benefit. When they challenge the request, the department head will declare a greater understanding of the issue than the team designated to do the job.

Another tactic is to find someone with another project who likes to 'nit pick', and encourage them to ask lots of questions about their project to the director of finance. When they get the answers to their questions, the arch-manipulator will encourage them to check the answers by making the request or similar requests again. They will find an agenda that is attractive to others, and dangle that in front of them to subtly encourage them to say nothing about their behaviour behind the scenes. The arch-manipulator will cross boundaries by ringing the director and people around them in the evenings and weekends, asking questions of little importance. When they protest, the arch-manipulator will suggest that their agenda is more important than theirs.

If this campaign is undertaken over a long period of time, the director of finance and the people around them will get busier, whilst at the same time their sense of being calm and centred would be knocked. They will be less able to keep their 'eyes on the ball'. As a result of this behaviour, the chances are that the finance director will lose their sense of control and will end up 'fighting so many fires' that the funding request goes through unchallenged. It is also interesting to note that the reason for the original request – to get additional funding – almost seems to get lost as the main focus for the activity is replaced with the need to win at all costs.

So what do you do if you have an arch-manipulator in your midst? The simple answer is to first recognise it is happening, and then not feed the behaviour in any way.

Manipulators are very skilled at causing a reaction, so when they push your 'buttons' to make you angry or defensive, calm down and use one of the assertiveness techniques of broken record, fogging, negative assertion and negative enquiry. This is easier said that done, since you will be put under extreme pressure to react. When you manage to stay in control, you will start to defuse their manipulations.

It may take a while for you to realise that whatever you say or do, you are not going to 'win', because you are not in an environment where logic or rational thinking has any relevance. You can then decide not to play the game, despite the very strong invitations you are receiving to engage in this behaviour. Once you are aware of the existence of this phenomenon, you can create your own strategies to deal with it.

Defusing the arch-manipulator – a step-by-step approach

Working with my clients, we were able to develop a step-by-step approach to defusing the impact of the arch-manipulator.

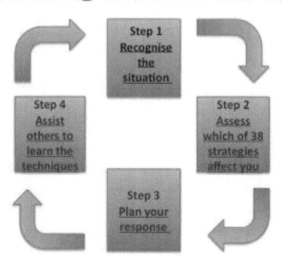

A Step by Step Approach to Defusing the Arch Manipulator

Step 1 Recognise the situation

Step 2 Assess which of 38 strategies affect you

Step 3 Plan your response

Step 4 Assist others to learn the techniques

- ▓ **Step 1:** Recognise that an arch-manipulator is in your environment
- ▓ **Step 2:** Assess which of the 38 Schopenhauer strategies affect you
- ▓ **Step 3:** Plan how you will respond to the arch-manipulator
- ▓ **Step 4:** Assist others to learn the defusing techniques

Step 1: Recognise that an arch-manipulator is in your environment (a very rare situation)

The first priority is to spot and identify the situation. This can be quite difficult when you find yourself surrounded by chaos that did not used to be there before. Do not try to convince other people of its existence. Defuse it yourself and then you will be in a strong position to assist other people to defuse it too. Be careful not to jump to conclusions over isolated incidents.

Step 2: Assess which of the 38 Schopenhauer strategies affects you (personally)

Arch-manipulators have a tendency to disempower you and disconnect you from your own sense of logic and integrity. Notice what 'buttons' they can press within yourself and others. For one client, it was his need to control his temper and his tendency not to take criticism well, combined with his compulsion to defend himself. For another, it was his need to maintain an audit trail of everything, so that he was able to defend against any criticism; this engaged him in spending valuable time putting in back-up systems and justifying his actions. For another, her personal standards meant that he only had to criticise a small element of her performance and it would send her into self-doubt and additional work.

This tiny group of individuals appears to like tying people in knots. They will plant little triggers in conversation, letters and emails, which will be almost unnoticed by others, but will have you reacting in the way they expect. They encourage you to make long explanations of the reasoning behind your behaviour, then criticise your logic. They will bury an almost imperceptible insult into their response that you feel forced to address. Then they will hook onto your unreasonable and irrational behaviour, and start to imply that you are not fit to do the job.

They will copy other people into your communications and suggest an implied criticism from you of another person. This will start you communicating with this third party directly, and either defending your behaviour or attacking theirs, when before the email you were interacting just fine. They will be aware that you are under deadline pressures and will imply that their work is more important and that you should drop what you are doing.

I think you get the general idea. So what do you do if you have a person like this is your midst? The simple answer is: do not feed the behaviour.

Step 3: Plan how you will respond to the arch-manipulator (to resist the very powerful desire to react to the stimulus that you are receiving)

Now this is going to sound easier than it actually is, but you need to stop using defending or attacking behaviour in response to their stimulus. From the chapter on assertiveness, the assertive toolkit of broken record, fogging, negative assertion and negative enquiry includes the most powerful techniques to keep you on course and avoid deflections. For example, if they have noticed that you tend to get drawn into the game when you are criticised, instead of long explanations that can be broken down piece by piece, give vaguer answers that suggest that everything is under control.

When you are personally criticised, use fogging statements, which suggest that you can understand why they may say that. In fact, you do understand why they might say that, of course, because you believe that they might be manipulative or unhinged. Go back and review the strategies you developed on page 55 to deal with deflections. The issues are the same, but because of the more subtle and pervasive challenges presented by the arch-manipulator, who tends to work at senior levels in organisations and groups, you might be knee-deep in chaos before you step back and consider what has changed in your environment.

The moment you start 'dancing to their tune' is the moment when you will get caught up in the whirlwind. So slow down, take a step back and review their behaviour and the way it is affecting you. Then stop reacting the way you have been doing. Generally become a bit more vague and unavailable. The more you can learn to regain your control, the more you will help others to do the same.

Step 4: Assist others (colleagues, friends and family) to identify the situation and to learn the defusing techniques

When you have managed to disempower the arch-manipulator and regained your sense of control, it is likely that others will become curious about how you managed to defuse the effects of the manipulator in your midst. You can then share your strategies with them, to enable them to do the same.

Before going on to the next section, you might find it helpful to review the chapter on how to become more assertive, since although the stimulus to respond is much more complex, when dealing with the arch-manipulator, the skills of responding to this stimulus are the same. In a sense, dealing with the arch-manipulator requires advanced skills of assertiveness.

Planning to defuse the arch-manipulator

Step 1: Recognise that the arch-manipulator is in your environment

Have you ever come across someone you could classify as an arch-manipulator?

What makes you think that?

What impact did they have on you?

What impact did they have on others in the organisation, group or family?

What happened to break the hold that they had on you and others?

Step 2: Assess which of the 38 Schopenhauer strategies affects you

Looking at the 38 common tricks and dodges of the controversial dialectic developed by Schopenhauer, which combination of the stratagems do you believe have been used on you in the past by someone you would consider to be an arch-manipulator?

Can you remember what they did or said to make you react?

How did you react when you experienced this behaviour?

What impact did this reaction have on the way you felt about yourself?

What did it feel like to be dancing to someone else tune?

Once you know what they are doing you can detach from it. The very fact of observing the process will help you to defuse the behaviour of the arch-manipulator.

Step 3: Plan how you will respond to the arch-manipulator

The irony of this step is that you are planning a response, which is to do nothing. This is a lot more difficult than it sounds since you will be under extreme provocation to react.

Looking at your previous responses in Step 2, what could you do (or not do) to react differently in the future?

What could you do to be more vague, non committal and unavailable?

How would you cope with responding in this way?

What would be the effect of behaving in this way?

How would you deal with the 'fall out' that the arch-manipulator creates when involving other people in the manipulation behind the scenes.

What sentence could you construct, which will dismiss their behaviour to other people? Keep this vague and non-committal. For example: 'He's an interesting character isn't he?' 'They do seem to expect a lot don't they?' 'Sometimes it is difficult to know where they are coming from, isn't it?'.

Step 4: Assist others to learn the defusing techniques

The strange thing about dealing with the arch-manipulator is that everyone will experience them differently since the arch-manipulator will 'press the buttons' of each person according to their specific areas of insecurity or weakness. For this reason it is hard for people to understand what is happening to them. They will, however, notice when a person is who used to being affected by the arch-manipulator has regained their sense of power and control, when they stop 'dancing to their tune'. At this point it is appropriate to share your disengagement techniques with them.

If a work colleague, group member or family friend asked you how you have managed to become calmer when the arch-manipulator is around, what would you say to them to help them to regain their sense of power and control?

Being centred

In the two years between writing the People Skills Revolution and writing this handbook, I have become interested in the idea of being centred. This has happened for two main reasons.

Firstly, I became aware that one of the key skills of the peacemaker is to understand the dramas of conflict and how they came about. They have to be able to do this in a way that they see the person behind the behaviour and be able to regard them in an 'I positive, you positive' manner. In other words, to realise that people are not their behaviour, and that learnt negative behaviour or game playing and manipulation can be unlearnt.

They also have to be able to detach from often very aggressive and manipulative behaviour and not get caught up in it, despite the very forceful stimulus they may receive to do this. If they failed to do this they will disable their ability to conciliate and make peace.

Secondly as I and my clients, gained a greater understanding of who 'we' are what 'we' stand for, we were also detaching from our own personal dramas. This made us, on the whole, much calmer but also made us much more aware of the stress that still remained in our lives. I also found that this greater sense of detachment enabled my clients to move into a much more observer role and they started to notice the areas of conflict. Then they seemed to use their intuition to get a better sense of when was the most appropriate time to act.

As a result of my growing interest in the part that being centred plays in our people skills, I started to meditate using a process that was recommended to me, which integrates the mind and the body. When my clients mentioned their need to find a way to deal with the considerable pressure they were under, and to help them to deal with people who continually attempted to manipulate them, as they moved into more senior roles, I also started to suggest this approach to them.

Meditative practice

Nearly every religious or spiritual tradition includes meditation in its daily practice. It can have a very powerful affect on quietening the mind and driving out negative thoughts. I use meditation to keep me calm, improve the mind/body link and develop my intuition. Recently I have also taken to recommending it to clients since I believe that the benefits are so powerful. I have included a very simple meditative practice here for you to follow, if you would like to do so.

Although there are a wide range of meditative practices available, the one that has worked best for me is the one advocated in 'Self Observation – the awakening of conscience – an owner's manual' by Red Hawk[14], who teaches at the University of Arkansas.

In this book, the author suggests that our thoughts are binary and that in any given situation we have the choice to select one of two options, for example, positive or negative, like or dislike, past or future. Once our basic positions about the world are selected, the mind selects only those *'bits which verify and validate its programmed perceptions of the world'*.

He goes on to explain that those perceptions form the basis of our belief systems, so that if we believe the world to be a cold, uncaring and unfriendly place, we accept and integrate only the information that reinforces this belief. I hope you can see the similarity between this idea and the approach to transforming negative beliefs set out on page 23.

In 'Self Observation', the author believes that tension in our body is linked to negative thoughts we have about ourselves. He suggests that in order for us to become aware of, and let go of our negative thoughts, we need to observe unnecessary tension in the body and then to relax it. To this, he adds four laws of self-observation:

1. Self observation without judgement (or interference).
2. Don't change what is observed.
3. Observe unnecessary tension in the body.
4. Self-honesty.

14 Hohm Press, 2009

Using this process for a few minutes a day, and gradually building up the amount of time you spend focusing on the tension in your body, will assist you to reduce negative thinking, improve the connection between your mind and body, enable you to feel more calm and centred and develop your intuition.

Meditative practice

Settle into a comfortable chair and close your eyes. Take some deep breaths in and out. Start to notice your breathing. Once you are into a settled breathing pattern, start to use your thoughts to scan your body to identify any areas of tension. When you find an area of tension in your body just move your attention there. Allow it to be and do not try to change it. As you focus your attention on the tension, it will start to change – you do not have to do anything to make this happen.

On day one, sit and observe the process for 15 minutes. Increase the time you meditate by a few minutes each day if you can.

Do the meditative process every day for a week and record your thoughts each day.

Day	Amount of time	Thoughts
Day 1		
Day 2		
Day 3		
Day 4		
Day 5		
Day 6		
Day 7		

If you have found this useful, include a meditation of around 30 minutes to 45 minutes into your daily routine.

As you begin to feel calmer and more centred, your intuition will increase and you will begin to sense areas of conflict and tension around, which may require your attention. In the past, you may have previously missed these situations or become embroiled in them.

You may also start to notice opportunities, or what I call 'magical moments'. These are times when the answers to questions become obvious to you or the right person appears at the right time to provide a new insight or solution. I believe that these opportunities are always around us, but when we are able to remain calm and observant, we are much more likely to notice and be able to take advantage of these situations.

What 'magical moments' have you experienced as a result of staying quiet, calm and centred?

Taking a stand – taking action

What action will you take as a result of reading this chapter?

When can you do this?

DO IT!
Report back

What happened?

What went well?

What would you do differently next time?

Reflection: In this section on taking a stand, we have covered a great deal of ground.

We have looked at who you are and what you stand for, introduced the concept of game playing and the drama triangle, explored how to identify and defuse the arch-manipulator and looked at how to centre yourself through meditation.

If you have completed the exercises in this chapter you may have experienced a powerful reaction to some of the ideas and concepts.

Take your time to integrate your thoughts before moving on to the next section. Jot down any reflections on these exercises below:

Remember: I hope that this chapter has helped you to see that not everything that someone does is about you. When working with others, we are entering a dynamic and what follows is not always what you might logically expect. In fact, much of what goes on between people is outside of their consciousness so it is important to have the skills to unpick events and understand them in order to plan different and more productive approaches.

Identifying and acknowledging that you may play the role of victim, persecutor or rescuer in your interactions with others and observing the process goes a long way in helping you to understand the underlying dynamics behind impoverished relationships. It also allows you to step out of the drama triangle and disengage from the game to adopt more healthy and more productive behaviours.

When I shared this chapter with the client who prompted me to read Schopenhauer's 'The Art of Controversy', he responded that he considered that the greatest success he had had with his own particular arch-manipulator was when he responded to an email that was a rant and tirade of threats that contained many Controversial Dialectic hooks by replying: 'I am sure he will do whatever he thinks appropriate'. He then went on to say that he had not experienced a reoccurrence of the problem since.

He also commented that he thought that this response sounded very similar to 'fogging' in the assertiveness toolkit.

Assertiveness skills are the underpinning skills, which form the foundation of all the other skills outlined in this book. On the point of taking a stand, you will need to practice them at an advanced level to help you to consistently and successfully achieve your goals and dreams one step at a time.

Getting in touch with who you are and what you stand for, clearing out old unproductive behaviours and replacing them with more healthy and effective behaviours is the key to not only achieving your own dreams but also assisting others to do the same.

Making peace

The final stage up the continuum of interpersonal skills is making peace. When I wrote the People Skills Revolution, the notion of making peace felt very nebulous and was based on the actions of Michael Young, who led the peace negotiations in South Africa, and Jonathan Powell and George J Mitchell, who helped to broker the peace settlement in Northern Ireland. I have decided to track this process using the step-by-step approach to peacemaking, since this was the original inspiration for the model.

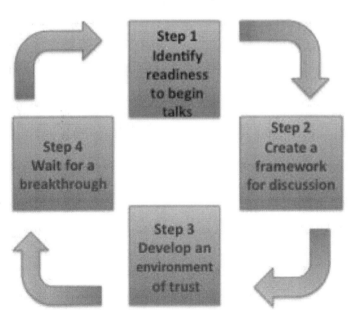

A Step by Step Approach to Making Peace

Step 1
Identify readiness to begin talks

Step 2
Create a framework for discussion

Step 3
Develop an environment of trust

Step 4
Wait for a breakthrough

- **Step 1:** Identify readiness to begin talks
- **Step 2:** Create a framework for discussion – and keep it going
- **Step 3:** Develop an environment of trust
- **Step 4:** Wait for a breakthrough

Although I believed that it was theoretically possible to move through the stages of the continuum to reach the point of making peace in a business environment rather than on the international stage, I did not actually know anyone who had achieved it.

Then the ex-client who suggested I wrote the original book, who has excellent interpersonal skills himself, kept mentioning that he was now working for a chief executive officer whose behaviour he just did not understand. What he described was a man who was able to turn up at the right moment, have a chat with people, and any conflict that was present just disappeared. This description got my interest and when looking for practical examples of behaviour for this book, I decided to see if I could meet this chief executive to find out what he was doing. I have included a fascinating transcript of our meeting since it documents his career, how he became a peacemaker and the process he went through to develop a peacemaking process that worked for him.

The example of peace making at an international level and the story of the CEO making peace at a business level are below. As you read the overview of the two case studies observe the similarities between the actions of an international peace maker who accidentally got thrust into the role and those of the chief executive officer.

Making peace – an international example

In the People Skills Revolution I highlight the work of Michael Young who was public affairs director of Consolidated Gold Fields (a mining company in South Africa). Young played a major role in facilitating the peaceful transition to black majority rule in South Africa after taking the stance that ideologically and intellectually, the Apartheid regime and the resulting virtual civil war, could not continue.

In an interview talking about his role in the peace process which was documented in the film Endgame broadcast in May 2009, Michael Young[15] highlighted the following actions, which led to the achievement of a successful outcome.

Step 1: Identify readiness to begin talks

1. Oliver Tambo, co-founder of the African National Congress challenged Michael Young to set a dialogue between the ANC and the Afrakaner establishment.

15 Adapted from an interview with Michael Young broadcast on the LastBroadcast.co.uk website 2009

2. The Chairman of Consolidated Gold Fields agreed, in principle, that Young could begin to try and forge links with the ANC in exile to see what they were like and what they wanted to happen.

3. Young met Oliver Tambo and asked him the question: 'What does a British company need to do to help with the resolution to the South African situation?'

   Oliver Tambo replied: 'Please help me to build a bridge. I need a bridge built to the regime in Pretoria.' Later on in the process, Thabo Mbeki said to Young that one of the ANC's greatest fears was that when the signals (of a readiness to talk) were coming from Pretoria, they would not be able to recognise them.

4. Young realised that it was critical for the ANC to gain some awareness of what the politicians in Pretoria were about, what were their tolerances and what were their fears. To do this, he looked at the power structure and identified people who were close to the centre of power, who also took the view that the *status quo* was not sustainable. These people also had to realise that something needed to be done and have the courage to follow that through.

5. Willie Esterhuyse, an Afrikaner social reformer and philosophy academic, had the courage to say 'yes I think what you are doing is right, and yes I'll come along on the journey with you'.

Step 2: Create a framework for discussion

6. Michael Young established two pre-conditions at the start of the talks. He told both sides that if they wanted to play games with this opportunity to make peace, he was not their man, and to avoid them 'playing to the gallery' he also insisted that the talks had to be held in secret. The group met on 12 occasions in Mells Park House in Somerset between 1985 and 1990.

7. Young suggested that with a bit of pushing and shoving it was relatively easy to get the parties to sit down and talk.

8. This second phase, creating a framework for discussions and managing the talks, was regarded by Young as almost as much of a challenge as getting them to meet. The difficulty here was to keep them focused, hold a substantive conversation, and make sure that they actually delivered a product. At first he was very prescriptive, but as the talks progressed, he moved from a chairman's role to a much more facilitatory role.

Step 3: Develop an environment of trust

9. In this facilitatory role the aim was to get the parties to talk to each other and to regard themselves as fellow South Africans. Once this shift happened he began to feel that they were going to achieve their objective.

10. As well as acting as a role model himself, Young took a number of actions to create an environment of trust. These included having excellent food and drink available during break times, and in the evening to promote a convivial atmosphere, encouraging walks in the grounds and making chance meetings between the warring parties more likely to happen by accommodating them in adjacent bedrooms.

Step 4: Wait for a breakthrough

11. The breakthrough happened when Thabo Mbeki deliberately took Willie Esterhuyse and the other whites through the command and control system of the ANC guerilla movement, and was effectively saying that the movement had its own limitations. Young suggests this was a very brave thing to do and unlocked the final element of trust that was so important to the process.

12. There were two more talks, after the release of Nelson Mandela, to keep the momentum going until Mandela and the unbanned ANC could sit down formally with President FW de Klerk to begin a formal, public process of negotiation.

13. The formal process itself moved very quickly, since discussions about unbanning, minority rights, what was to happen to Mandela, how riots could be avoided and the nature of the post-Apartheid economy, had all been gone through in great depth during the Mells Park process.

It was interesting that a very similar process was adopted in Northern Ireland when peace was achieved in May 2007.

Making peace – a practical example

As I mentioned earlier in the chapter, although I was aware of the peacemaking negotiations that took place in South Africa and Northern Ireland, I was not aware of anyone acting in a similar fashion in a business environment. Then I was presented with the opportunity to speak to a chief executive who I believed had these skills and was working at this stage.

I found the conversation I had with him fascinating at many levels, so I have decided to include the interview in its entirety in this chapter on making peace because his story essentially tracks the sequence of skill development, which led him to become a peacemaker in a business environment.

Bear in mind that prior to the meeting, I had sent the CEO the People Skills Revolution so that he was aware what the discussion would be about. I had also taken a copy of the continuum of interpersonal skills with me so that we could refer to it during the interview.

The first question I asked him was: 'Does the continuum of interpersonal skills resonate with you?' To this he replied: 'Would a potted history of my career help'? I said it would, and this is how the rest of the interview unfolded.

'I was a Secondary Modern boy who came from a council estate, who had been written off at 11. Somehow I realised I had an ability to pass exams with a minimum of homework.

'If I have a style, it is that I do not think I am superior to anyone. I was encouraged to get an education and at the time I got a full grant. My parents knew nothing about education and were not in a position to advise me, although they did give me a lot of encouragement. They realised I could do something different and allowed me to do that. Not many people went to university at the time.

'A lot of people who I grew up with denied their past, but I felt "I am what I am and I can feel confident in myself". I am also quite shy.

'At University I studied Economics. It felt easy, there was no one standing in my way and saying I couldn't do it.'

At this point I asked if his family had good interpersonal skills and he said 'no'.

He then continued:

'At 17, I spent five months in hospital and when I left university I decided to apply for an NHS finance traineeship. I did this for a number of reasons; they had a fully funded training scheme, I remembered my time in hospital and I think I felt comfortable in that environment since I was able to talk their language. Also my career has never been just a job to me. I have a passionate belief about trying to make it better. I think we are a very fortunate generation to have the NHS and we tend to take it for granted.

'I had two life changing events – going to university and when I left the Health Service and went to work for one of the world's leading professional services organisations.

'I took up finance because I am good at numbers, but I don't do numbers for numbers sake. They are not inanimate objects and I ask myself: "What can I do with the numbers?"

'After a few jobs in the Health Service, I arrived at a prestigious hospital on the south coast and I ended up a bit disillusioned. I was in charge of the capital programme, and although the buildings were falling to bits, the money was being spent on flashy bits of kit. There was also some particularly bad behaviour from the consultants. The leader spent his time running around in circles and trying to keep everyone happy.

I was marketable and qualified, and decided I wanted to leave. I liked the professional services company, I liked the people and I liked the status of the job. I stayed there four years. It was an interesting experience and I think I became more assertive at this point.

'I can be shy but I am always honest. I apply assertiveness attached to honesty. I don't bullshit and I don't give them the answers they want. I tell people the answer is no and then I then I tell them why'.

I questioned whether it was the experience at the hospital on the south coast that had made him more assertive. He said: 'yes, early on in my career, I saw what was happening and thought about what I would do differently. The other guy did not "bite the bullet".'

He then continued: 'Leaving the Health Service and joining the private company gave me a whole set of new skills. I became good at empathy. I had a good knowledge base and I could relate well to clients – I could get a lot of information out of them. I didn't do an influencing skills course as such, but I did a process consulting course, which is similar and I found out I was good at it.

'When you are shy, it's a box of tricks and I have always been reflective. Everyone can have their own style of leadership. I think I am subtler; I grow on people.

'At the professional services company I took on the job of assessing the viability of hospitals on behalf of the Department of Health for a new purchaser/provider model, which was being introduced. At the time, I was getting married and wanted a greater degree of stability in my life, so I decided to join the clients. I became a director of finance in a hospital in Kent. It was a lucky break, which gave me a high profile and I knew how to "pass the bar".

'As director of finance I did a lot of project work including managing the application to become a trust. Since it was moving *towards a purchaser/provider model, there was a lot of negotiation. I learnt that you did not have to win every battle. I knew where the "red lines" were. I knew what I needed to deliver and where I could not give anything up. Short of those "red lines" I was aware that you need to give up things that were peripheral and that these things might not be peripheral for the other person.*

'In fact I might create a situation where I had to give something up so that I could demonstrate that I was ready to compromise. I used psychology to enable the other person to feel that they were getting something out of it and had achieved a successful negotiation.

'I am very fortunate that I can hone in and decide what are the critical things that need to be delivered and know what I can give up. I can cut to the chase very quickly and grasp what is important with minimal briefing. The concept of "red lines" was used in the professional services company and I found this idea very useful. I learnt to get a clear grasp of the priorities in an organisation. I knew what to pull out and synthesise into "red lines" and to know where they were.'

I then showed the CEO, Carl Jung's Psychological Types, Intuitor, Thinker, Feeler and Sensor model. He felt that although he started off as a Thinker, early on in his career he realised that people were an important part of the process. He is now very conscious of switching styles and how he communicates. He said he was conscious of all elements of his communication approach. He then continued.

'Most people see me as a natural, but there is a lot of psychological thinking behind what they see. When I approach people, I do my

homework. *If you understand what their private concerns are, you know where they are coming from. I have never had a performance development plan in my life, but my whole life is a performance development process. I am aware that I think all my skills have happened by accident, but when you look back at it, it has all been a conscious decision. The downside of these skills is that sometimes people say that I am difficult to "read". I am not a "one trick pony" – if you have someone who is aggressive and they are consistently aggressive, they are not difficult to "read".*

'*I think the idea that there is a transition between negotiation and conciliation is true. You need to give in things (and I have done it deliberately) in order to be conciliatory. It is not good to win everything. You need to see the value of the longer-term relationship.*

'*During my time as director of finance, I was doing less finance work and more of other things. I had got bored in finance and wanted to take on other challenges. I angled to be a chief executive and applied for a couple of jobs, which I did not get. I was told I was not "'touchy feely" enough, so made a conscious effort to be a little cuddlier.*

'*I was advised to do another role in another organisation, which was not finance. Taking on a director of operations position, I was conscious that it was a stepping stone to the CEO role. I took this as an opportunity to hone all my people skills.*

'*Then I got parachuted into a trust, which was recovering from a scandal, as chief executive. The previous person had been sidelined and the executive team were appalled by what had happened. It* was an incendiary situation where someone said "do you realise people hate you?"

'It was clear that they thought I was going to "slash and burn", and I was criticised heavily. It took me three months to establish myself into role and to gain the loyalty and trust of the organisation. I achieved this without bringing anyone else in and I used the team I had.

'In taking up the role, my strategy was to talk to people to find out where they were coming from. I talked to the consultants and spotted key players who were not necessarily the most senior in the organisation, but people who I felt could make a difference. I am good at spotting people you can trust quickly and identifying their strengths. I am also good at spotting peoples' "Achilles heel".

'I am aggressive with the statement "always read the signals" and sometimes, of course, you will make the wrong call. Unless you are willing to make the wrong call you are not pushing yourself enough. I feel that I am empowering people to fail – I believe that people should act right on the boundary – then they would take more risks.

'I will admit I was scared rigid on my first day. You think you know what you are doing but you don't. I don't feel the need to know everything, but I do need to know someone who does. I am proud of my ability to identify those people. My style is to warm people up – I do not see myself as an "impact player".

'Then I moved into an organisation that had been "run into the ground" with a £21m deficit. This was an extremely political *environment where they were politically killing each other. I realised I needed friends and people who could help. I needed support and "air cover" particularly if I was doing something different. To create "friends" I always did want I said I would do, established a track record and presented myself as someone they could do business with.*

'It was here that I realised that if I became too emotionally involved in the organisation that I would lose my perspective. When you fight for everything for the organisation, when it comes to the end, you end up losing.

'Stucturally I did not make a load of people redundant, although I did take a personal interest in moving people on. Six months later, I had a new team in place and "no blood on the carpet", without it costing any money. As long as you have a game plan and stick to it – that is being decisive – that is true even if people are "baying for blood", which can make it very difficult.

'I treat people fairly and give them the benefit of the doubt. I assume they are okay until they prove otherwise. The worst mistake I made was to give someone too many chances. I spent nine months and a lot effort trying to pull it around. When it did not work, I was disappointed when I got abuse instead of thanks. I realised that there was an element of truth in the criticism that they felt that I was stringing them along and that you may be doing people a favour by acting quickly.

'At the same time as sorting out the executive team, I introduced objectives and an appraisal system, which is the simplest way of doing the job and allowing people to take responsibility.'

At this point I asked him how he approached conciliation with people who were in conflict. He found it difficult to give a specific example because he said he did this everyday and almost did not notice when he was doing it. Then I asked him about his process, and he said that earlier in his career there had been so much going on in warring organisations that you had to do something. He started experimenting with different approaches. There had been a lot of trial and error, but eventually he found a process that had worked.

Coincidentally the structure he had stuck with was the same recommended in the People Skills Revolution, which is based on the ACAS (Abritration and Conciliation Service) approach. This involves meeting the two parties individually to identify their issues, developing an agenda and then bringing the two people together to find an effective compromise. This is what he said about his process.

'When two people are at loggerheads, I get them to expand, and explain that neither of them is necessarily wrong and my aim is to help them to achieve a compromise. I get to know the people to find out what makes them tick, and find out where it might be possible to do a deal. In doing this, I state that it is critical for them to explain the issues, so that the other party understands where they are coming from. Then I work with them in a joint meeting to identify a compromise that they can both sign up to.'

Looking at the continuum of interpersonal skills, I then asked the CEO if the 'Taking a stand' stage had any relevance to him. He agreed it did and said:

'Taking a stand is about resisting pressure. There are people

*without honour wreaking havoc around an organisation – it's often
about dealing with them.*

*'Also when I was parachuted into the organisation to sort out the
scandal, I was told what to do by the people above me, which I
resisted. It was a risk, but I also figured "I was the only game in
town".*

*'I do have a moralistic side to me. I believe in treating people fairly
and treating people how you would like to be treated yourself at
all levels. I have a very developed sense of fairness. Taking a stand
can be difficult. At one of the hospitals, we were asked to host an
Independent Treatment Centre, which would take work away from
the NHS, and there was a huge financial bung attached to it. I
made myself unpopular by saying it was economic madness and
banging on about it at the Department of Health. In the end, they
did relent, it never happened, and I managed to attract additional
funds to our organisation.*

*'I surprised myself about how preoccupied I got about it. There
is a danger you will lose your edge but there were key principles
involved in all of it.*

*'I did have sleepless nights and got wound up about the sheer
gargantuan stupidity of it. Taking a stand for what you believe
in becomes a way of life. I don't intervene on everything. I very
much "keep my powder dry". There is "only so much fuel in the
tank" so you need to use your interventions sparingly. Sometimes
you have to "get out of your pram" to have more impact. I am
conscious of doing that. I used to think that this was more random
and rationalised it. Now I am conscious that I do it deliberately – I*

know exactly when I am going to lose my temper and this has the greatest impact when I do not do it very often.'

I then went on to ask about the making peace stage, and we had a brief chat about the agreements that were made in South Africa and Northern Ireland, which were documented in the People Skills Revolution. I was fascinated by the CEO's response to this question.

'The most important skill of the CEO is not about identifying what is the right thing to do. It is all about timing and spotting when the time is right to act. I learnt this when I worked in the private sector, when I was asked the question: "When is the right time for a large department store chain to have a sale. Do you have it when people have got lots of money, or when they are short of it?"

'Most people think that it is when money is tight, but in fact, people buy when they have money in their pockets. If you have a sale when you notice that people don't have money, no one will buy. Having sales is all about timing. So whatever you are selling, you have to catch people when they want to buy.

'We had some orthopedic surgeons who were very disaffected because their job plans were scuppered. The surgical rotas were not working well and the service itself was not working. They could not continue like that, but you have to create the space and timing to make a meaningful fist of it.

'I could have tackled it head on but waited for the time when they said: "we can't continue with this". It took six months for them to get to a place where they were prepared to give something up in order to make it better. At this point anything is better than what

currently exists and they came to the negotiating table wanting to do a deal rather insisting on a lot of preconditions.

'The critical thing here is spotting the right time. You can often have the right answer at the wrong time.

'You can also create the right time too. I can be a bit cynical, sending someone who understands what we are doing, to go out and stir things up a bit, which enables me to "keep my own powder dry". This helps to sew the seeds of getting the timing right. I see this very much as "shading the odds" and bringing the timing together.'

In the dispute between the surgeons and the management, he had already tried conciliation and had identified the issues as follows. The surgeons perceived that they:

- felt that the reconfiguration had been done to them,
- had no input,
- had no power to do their work,
- were 'run ragged',
- were not able to give the best quality of care,
- were powerless to do something about it.

The management perceived that:

- the surgeons don't take any notice,
- the surgeons had caused the problems themselves,
- they were not willing to talk about it,
- there was no solution,

   ▓ *they would not come up with any alternatives,*

   ▓ *it was all their fault.*

'In my role as peacemaker, it is critical not to be seen as part of the management. I want to have a proper arbitration process and "keep my powder dry".

'In order to make peace I got them all in a room and told them that the situation was unacceptable and can't be allowed to continue, and asked them "what are you going to do about it?"

'They reacted with a degree of shock; the surgeons expected me to tow the management line and to tell them what to do. The management side did not like it because they felt that it was giving into the surgeons.

'I empowered them to sort it out for themselves. The two sides got their act together. The consultants visited other places to see what other trusts were doing and came back with a proposal. The management did not like this initially, but since the timing was right, they understood that they would actually benefit if they accepted the solution and they took it on board.'

Showing him the step-by-step approach to peacemaking, he agreed that this was a similar process to the one he used with the surgeons and the management.

A Step by Step Approach to Making Peace

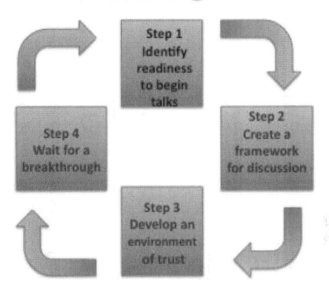

- **Step 1**: Identify readiness to begin talks
- **Step 2**: Create a framework for discussion
- **Step 3**: Develop an environment of trust
- **Step 4**: 'Wait for a breakthrough'

Step 1: Identify the readiness to begin talks

It was clear that the CEO waited until the situation had become unbearable for both parties before taking action. He also said that he had helped this along by sending a colleague along to stir things up a bit with the surgeons, and I would suspect make them more aware of their dissatisfactions. When he felt that the time was right, he called the meeting. He did this in the knowledge that they would be prepared to relent on some of the issues that previously they had stated were non-negotiable.

Step 2: Create a framework for discussion

When he facilitated the meeting, he established their readiness to enter talks and said that the situation could not continue and must be changed. He brought them to the discussion table at just the right time and acted in the role of independent arbitrator. Whilst he allowed them to vent some of their concerns, he was clear at all times that they had to develop a process that would lead to a solution to the problems they faced.

He set the scene that it was not about who was right or wrong. Instead he created a no blame environment where the focus at all times was on the way forward.

Step 3: Develop an environment of trust

The health service culture can be a place where game playing and arch-manipulation thrives. The CEO had already established a relationship with both parties when he met them individually to identify their issues in the hope of achieving a conciliated agreement. At this point, he would have resisted a great deal of pressure from both sides to become part of the game by acting as a rescuer, persecutor or victim. When he resisted taking on any of these roles, he avoided becoming a player in the drama triangle, or a puppet of the arch-manipulator. The CEO very clearly positioned himself as an independent facilitator, even before the meeting started. He also demonstrated that he would create a safe environment where people would be protected from the attacks from others in the room.

Sitting around the table, they knew that they could not manipulate their way out of the situation or continue to blame. I believe his ability to defuse arch-manipulation and avoid becoming part of the game, played a very significant role in his ability to get them to engage in the process. Also, by modeling the behaviour himself, he was able to demonstrate to others that you can treat people with equality and fairness without having to get caught up in the drama. He showed that you could keep focused on the issue, which was that the situation had to change, and treated every other intervention as a distraction.

In making peace, the impact of the facilitator as role model cannot be underestimated. The need to create an environment of trust, which reassures the warring parties that the process will be safe, is critical to success.

If the peacemaker has an 'Achilles heel', the warring parties will look for it, find it, and attempt to exploit it. As soon they respond to the considerable pressure they will receive to react to this stimulus, they become part of the problem rather than part of the solution.

Step 4: Wait for a breakthrough

In the example with the surgeons in the NHS, it was clear that even the CEO was surprised by the reaction of the parties. The surgeons had taken the unusual step of going out of their way to visit other trusts to find a solution to the problem, and that was in the process of being accepted. The CEO had empowered them to step out of the drama and gave them back the sense of control that they perceived that they had lost as a result of the reconfiguration.

It is unlikely that once both sides have achieved this success that they would return to the behaviour that had proved to be so destructive both to their colleagues and to the service as a whole. Once you are able to step out of the drama triangle, most people do not want to go back, and it is the behaviour of the peacemaker that leads the way.

Making of the peacemaker

This interview illustrates a number of factors about the making of the peacemaker, which are worth highlighting.

The CEO agreed that his people skills development followed the continuum of interpersonal skills approach, even if he had no awareness of an underlying process. More specifically:

- He was prepared to adapt his approach according to the situation.
- If what he was doing was not working, he tried something different. This is the same approach as the arch-manipulator but combined with his highly principled approach, the same strategy becomes a highly effective force for peace.
- The stability of his success encouraged him to learn new skills and achieve further success.
- The concept of 'I positive, you positive' and treating people equally, fairly and with respect, underpinned all his behaviour.
- He had decided early on in his career that the inability to say 'no' allowed people to run rings around you. He managed to avoid this happening by saying a firm 'no' combined with honesty.
- He consciously adapted his style to who he was talking to and was very aware of his ability to do this.
- He regarded knowing where the 'red lines' are and timing as the key to effective negotiation, conciliation and making peace.

- He had developed a strategic mind and held a long-term view of events.
- He still regarded himself as shy, despite his confidence in a wide range of interpersonal situations.
- He clearly followed processes he knew worked and enjoyed increasing his level of skill as he achieved positions of increasing seniority in his career.
- He empowered others to develop these skills and resolve their differences.
- He created frameworks to encourage dialogue and ensured that the parties remained solution focused.
- He maintained low visibility and did not feel he had to be an impact player to make a difference in his organisation.
- He regarded his ability to cut to the chase and identify the key issues as a major component in his successful approach.
- He experienced an increasing level of calmness, control and centreness as his skills progressed, and felt he only lost his temper consciously and only for effect.

Taking action – becoming a peacemaker

Looking around your organisation, groups or family, which parties are constantly at war regardless of any attempts to assist them to conciliate?

In your view, what are the key issues that are the root cause of the problems they are experiencing?

People move away from their current position of pain when the pain of staying where they are outweighs the pain of moving towards a different position. What pain do you think both parties might be experiencing in their current position?

What could happen to increase the pain of both parties in their current position?

What indicators could you look for to know when both parties might be ready to sit around a negotiation table?

In the meantime, how could you, as a possible peacemaker, build a relationship of trust with both parties prior to their decision to enter into a peacemaking process?

Peacemakers have a clear agenda for the meeting, and then use that clear agenda to create a safe place for discussions. What framework for discussions could you create for these two parties?

Peace happens when both parties start to see each other as part of the solution, rather than part of the problem. What activities could you create that are low risk, which would encourage the warring parties to see each other as people rather than representatives of particular groups or factions?

How would you deal with the fact that you are facilitating a process with a clear framework, and creating an environment that is conducive to peace, but have no control over whether peace happens?

What could you say to the representatives of both parties, which would encourage them to engage in a peacemaking process?

How could you model the behaviour you would like both parties to adopt when they come around the negotiating table?

What would you personally gain out of achieving a peace between the two parties?

What could you do about this situation to move this further towards peacemaking now?

When could you do this?

DO IT!
Report back

Which of the actions discussed above did you take?

What reactions did you experience?

What would you do differently next time?

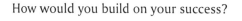

How would you build on your success?

What is the next step?

Reflection: The decision to act as peacemaker should not be made lightly. It is about being able to read the signs when the parties signal their readiness to make peace. It is also about building a relationship of trust, creating (and adhering to) a problem-solving framework and having the interpersonal skills to keep all the participants safe in the process. It should not be attempted unless you feel that you have a real chance of success, and the benefits of doing it far outweigh the risks of not doing it.

At this point you will be working on the boundary between success and failure and pushing yourself very hard in the process.

This chapter is as much about you understanding your own skills and your own readiness to step in to make peace as it is about the behaviour of the people in opposition.

What have been your reactions to reading about Michael Young and how he played a significant part in facilitating the peaceful transition to black majority rule in South Africa?

What have been your reactions to reading about the CEO featured in this chapter?

What have been your reactions to the demands placed on the peacemaker?

What further skills or experience do you need before you would feel comfortable to take on this role?

Remember: In this chapter on peacemaking, I have tried to highlight that with the appropriate sophisticated people skills, underpinned by assertiveness, influencing, negotiation and conciliation, more people can progressively become peacemakers provided they are prepared to take a stand to assist those in conflict.

Although I believe that very few people are currently operating at this level, the very practical example from the CEO shows that this level of skill development and readiness to act is possible in a business environment.

I hope that this chapter has served to illustrate that major significant change is not only possible in individuals, to assist them to take up the challenge of becoming a peacemaker, but also that significant change is also possible in the people who they come into contact with and have an impact on.

This section demonstrates not just that individual positive change is possible, but with the complete set of sophisticated skills developed in a step-by-step manner, cultural change is possible between countries, in a business environment, in interest groups, and in families.

At the end of the interview I thanked the CEO for sharing his thoughts with me and being prepared to share them in this handbook. I also asked him something I had been asking a number of finance directors and chief executives.

My question was: 'Do you think that the People Skills Revolution could be used as an organisational development tool in your organisation?' He agreed that it could be used in this way, and that the key to this approach would be timing and getting the executive team involved. This would be important since, from his experience as well as mine, senior management can scupper initiatives, which challenge the *status quo,* even if they are popular further down the organisation.

Starting a revolution

Revolutions have to start somewhere. I believe that the skills outlined in this book could transform the way that people interact with each other, one to one, in organisations, in groups, in families, at a national level, and on the international stage.

Those who have developed these skills, or are moving in this direction in a consistent, step-by-step manner, become the best ambassadors for the approach but the number of people performing this role at present are relatively small. They include my clients, participants on my courses, readers of the original book and people like the CEO described in the chapter on Making Peace, who have found and followed their own personal development paths.

But it is not just about having the answers to a number of the problems facing people today. As the CEO would say, it is also about having the right answers at the right time. At the moment, I believe that manipulators and drama kings and queens have the upper hand, leaving the rest of us bemused about what is happening. As a result we are gradually loosing our sense of control, without quite knowing why. It suits a lot of people to keep us like that. It is not until we start becoming aware of what is happening, noticing the behaviour that maintains the *status quo,* and challenging it with our people skills that society will become a more pleasant and productive place to be.

What needs to happen is for all the nice, cuddly, honest, often shy people to learn the people skills to achieve their goals and dreams in a direct manner, starting with assertiveness. I believe that when this starts to happen, others will notice and begin to say 'I want what they are having'. When this process reaches a 'tipping point', more people will be attracted to join the revolution. This is a revolution where nearly everyone has something to gain, and a tiny minority have something to lose.

Sometimes it feels like I am having a sale when people do not have money in their pockets. I believe the ideas in this book will 'catch', either when people see the success that others are having, or when their own sense of dissatisfaction with the current situation is heightened. For this to happen, awareness needs to be raised about what manipulators do, and people need to understand and be able to step out of the dynamics behind the drama triangle.

A major shift is likely to occur when more readers experience the radical, positive change in behaviour and outcomes that the ideas in the book can bring about, and when other people observe this happening.

To increase the nucleus of people on this journey, I have decided to include a section for groups to follow and an approach to using the People Skills Revolution as an organisational development tool.

People Skills Revolution – a group development approach

Since training budgets are tight at the best of times, and it is difficult to fit extra activities into busy lives, I have developed a process for groups that divides the content of the handbook into 22 two-hour sessions, which can be organised over a period of six months to a year. These have been designed in such a way that they can be run with or without a trained facilitator. They can also be bolted together to run five one-day workshops on assertiveness, influencing, negotiation, conciliation, taking a stand and making peace.

A note about the group development approach. I believe in treating people as intelligent, capable adults who can change their behaviour to achieve better results. For this reason, the 22 sessions are fast paced and cover a lot of ground. From experience, I believe that people can handle this degree of stretch, particularly when they and other group members achieve better results as they weave through the process. The sessions represent guidelines and suggestions.

It is hoped that the groups that form will then continue to meet to develop their people skills further and increase the impact they have on their immediate environments and the wider society.

Session 1: Introductions to the programme

Welcome and introductions
Introduction to the People Skills Revolution
The continuum of interpersonal skills

The beliefs and skills approach
Where are you now, where you want to be, and how are you going to get there?
Changing negative beliefs
Intersession work: Use changing negative beliefs approach to review beliefs

Session 2: Principles of assertiveness

Group check-in
Review of intersession work: Changing negative beliefs
Basic principles of assertiveness
Step-by-step approach to assertiveness
Tools of assertiveness
Saying 'no' and demonstration
Intersession work: Observe situations where you would like to be more assertive

Session 3: Assertiveness in practice

Group check-in
Review of intersession work: Observe situations when want to be more assertive
How people get recognition
Assertiveness practice
Giving constructive feedback
Giving constructive feedback practice
Intersession work: Notice situations when you would like to give constructive feedback and try it out

Session 4: Assertiveness in action and role modeling

Group check-in
Review of intersession work: Experiences of giving constructive feedback
Review experience of applying assertiveness techniques
Intersession work: Identify a role model who is an excellent influencer and observe the skills and qualities they display

Session 5: Introduction to influencing

Group check-in
Review of intersession work: Qualities and skills of the excellent influencer
Step-by-step approach to influencing

Influencing verses manipulation
How to build rapport
Intersession work: Practice building rapport

Session 6: Influencing through understanding others

Group check-in
Review of intersession work: Experiences of building rapport
Establishing credibility
Psychological types
Intersession work: Practice establishing credibility and identifying the four psychological types.

Session 7: Influencing by establishing your credibility

Group check-in
Review of intersession work: Experiences of establishing credibility and identifying psychological types
Types of power
Hierarchy of language
Intersession work: Put elements together to start establishing credibility

Session 8: Influencing in practice

Group check-in
Review of intersession work: Experiences of establishing credibility
Making a request
Follow up
Influencing practice
Intersession work: Put elements together to start influencing others

Session 9: Developing an influencing strategy

Group check-in
Review of intersession work: Outcomes of influencing in real-life situations
The power of chats
How to become a better listener
How to become a better questioner
Developing an influencing strategy
Intersession work: Take action to influence people

Session 10: Influencing clinic

Check-in
Review of intersession work - Experience of applying influencing approach techniques
Integration of learning
Intersession work: Interview someone whom you consider to be an excellent negotiator to find out what skills and qualities are required to achieve a win-win outcome.

Session 11: Introduction to negotiation

Check-in
Review of intersession work: Skills and qualities of an excellent negotiator
Basic principles of negotiation
Step-by-step approach to negotiation
How to prepare for negotiation
The debate stage checklist
Intersession work: Prepare a negotiation grid and debate checklist for a negotiation exercise

Session 12: Negotiation in practice I

Check-in
Review of intersession work: Reactions to preparing negotiation grid and debate checklist
Listening and questioning revisited
Negotiation practice – job offer
Negotiation debrief
Intersession work: Begin to notice negotiation opportunities

Session 13: Negotiation in practice II

Check-in
Review of intersession work: What negotiation opportunities did you identify?
Subtleties of negotiation – use of pause
Negotiation practice – business example
Negotiation debrief
Intersession work: Review your outcomes against other people's and work out why they were better or worse than your counterparts

Session 14: Negotiation clinic

Check-in

Review of intersession work: What makes the difference between average and exceptional negotiators?

Negotiation integration

Intersession work: Consider being at the cusp between negotiation and conciliation. What would make you move from being an effective negotiator to be interested in becoming a conciliator?

Session 15: Introduction to conciliation

Check-in

Review of intersession work

Basic principles of conciliation

A step-by-step approach to conciliation

Advanced communication skills

How to build trust

Clarifying the purpose of conciliation

Intersession work: Talk to people who have been angry or upset and ask their permission to help them to clarify the reasons for their concerns

Session 16: Conducting conciliation meetings

Check-in

Review of intersession work: Experiences of talking to people in distress

How to translate concerns into an agenda

Conciliation practice

Intersession work: Observe the behaviour of others to see why conflict might develop

Session 17: Conciliation in practice

Check-in

Review of intersession work: Observed reason for conflict

What did you learn about people from learning about conciliation?

How to avoid conflict from happening in the first place

Intersession work: What can you do to offer your services as a conciliator?

Session 18: Taking a stand and dreaming the dream

Group check-in
Review of intersession work
Taking a stand and dreaming your dreams – a personal inventory
Game playing and the drama triangle
A step-by-step approach to stepping out of the drama triangle
Intersession work: Observe the drama triangle in operation in real life situations

Session 19: Resisting pressure from arch-manipulators

Group check-in
Review of intersession work: Observations of the drama triangle in real life
Who is an arch-manipulator?
The 38 stratagems of the controversial dialectic or arch-manipulator
A step-by-step approach to defusing the arch-manipulator
How to plan your response to the arch-manipulator
Assisting other people to learn the techniques
Intersession work: Notice when you allow people and events to pull you off centre and what impact it has on your performance and sense of well being

Session 20: Being centred

Group check-in
Review of intersession exercise: Experiences of being pulled off centre by events or people. Why did this happen?
Meditation practice
Visualisation practice
Intersession work: What have your learnt about yourself and others from completing the section on taking a stand?

Session 21: Introduction to making peace

Group check-in
Review of intersession exercise: What have you learnt about yourself and others when taking a stand?
The step-by-step approach to making peace
What skills do you have to become a peacemaker?
What are your motivations to become a peacemaker?

What are your opportunities to become a peacemaker?

How would you begin a peacemaking process?

Intersession work: Where are you now, where do you want to be and how are you going to get there?

Session 22: Where are you now?

Group check-in

Review of the programme: Where are you now, where do you want to be, and how are you going to get there?

Decisions regarding the future of the group

Designing a new structure

People Skills Revolution – an organisational development approach

Since writing the original People Skills Revolution, I have become aware of the potential to use the step-by-step approach to developing sophisticated people skills as an organisational development tool. I believe the approach, if developed from the bottom up at a 'grass roots' level and supported from the 'top' as a strategic initiative, would substantially contribute to a high-performance organisation. This could be achieved with a minimum of cost and achieve huge benefits in terms of improved customer service, clear focus, reduced stress and increased profits.

The defining characteristics of such a culture would be a focus on production rather than drama, and the creation of an enjoyable, 'can do' attitude to work. This in turn would engender great customer service, and significantly increase the client base, leading to greater profit and satisfaction levels.

From my previous experience of organisational development, it has become clear to me that a very small minority of senior managers can sabotage an initiative when operating at board level or just below it. When I mentioned using the group approach to organisational culture change, I was surprised that the chief executives and the directors of finance I was speaking to had all considered how to use the approach in their own environments. All of them suggested that the book and the techniques would be most useful when used alongside coaching for their senior managers.

I added to this by saying that from my experience, once people had started on the approach, and had access to the People Skills Revolution techniques, most people only seemed to need three sessions at monthly intervals before they became 'hooked on the success' that these step-by-step approaches and strategies can provide.

As an interesting addendum to this idea, one director, who had known me and had been familiar with the People Skills Revolution approach for many years, suggested that as a director of finance, he would only offer the opportunity of coaching to the people in the organisation that would benefit from it. He was keen to ensure that at board level, those who had a tendency to become entrenched in organisational politics and games did not get the chance to develop the skills that would enable them to do this in a more sophisticated and dramatic way.

Which brings me back to the point that the People Skills Revolution is a step-by-step approach to empower people to develop sophisticated people skills that will benefit them, the groups they are a part of, the organisations they work in, and finally the wider community.

Next steps

Pamela Milne is Director of Solutions Unlimited, a consultancy dedicated to bringing about fundamental change in individuals, teams and organisations.

For more information on People Skills Revolution change programmes or to contact the author, visit the Solutions Unlimited website www.Solutionsunlimited.co.uk